Metro Litho
Oak Forest, IL 60452

DATE DUE

AMERICA the BEAUTIFUL

INDIANA

By R. Conrad Stein

Consultants

R. Dale Ogden, Curator of History, Indiana State Museum and Historic Sites

William R. Wepler, Curator of Anthropology, Indiana State Museum and Historic Sites

Robert L. Hillerich, Ph.D., Bowling Green State University, Bowling Green, Ohio

CHILDRENS PRESS ®
CHICAGO

The Narrows covered bridge, in Turkey Run State Park, was built in 1882.

Project Editor: Joan Downing
Associate Editor: Shari Joffe
Design Director: Margrit Fiddle
Typesetting: Graphic Connections, Inc.
Engraving: Liberty Photoengraving

Library of Congress Cataloging-in-Publication Data

Stein, R. Conrad.
   America the beautiful. Indiana / by R. Conrad
Stein.
     p.   cm.
   Includes index.
   Summary: Introduces the geography, history,
government, economy, industry, culture, historic
sites, and famous people of the Hoosier State.
   ISBN 0-516-00460-3
   1. Indiana—Juvenile literature. [1. Indiana.]
I. Title.
F526.3.S74   1990
977.2—dc20   89-25281
                                   CIP
                                    AC

This Indiana stone quarry has become a popular swimming hole.

TABLE OF CONTENTS

Chapter 1

WELCOME TO INDIANA

WELCOME TO INDIANA

Indiana is called the Hoosier State. How the word *Hoosier* originated is the subject of endless debate. Some historians believe the nickname dates back to log-cabin days, when it was customary for Indianans to answer a knock on the door with the words "who's yere?"—which was shortened to Hoosier. Other experts claim the term comes from certain iron-fisted frontiersmen (hushers) who were so feared they silenced a room simply by entering. Whatever its origin, Hoosier is the most famous nickname of all the states. A person who can remember no other state nickname knows that Indiana is the Hoosier State.

Indiana is a land of great variety, and it boasts a golden past. It has been the home of five vice-presidents and one president. An unusual number of writers have come from the Hoosier State. The nation's most popular automobile race—the Indianapolis 500—is held every Memorial Day weekend in the Hoosier capital. Indiana's economy embraces the smoky steel mills of Gary as well as the rich farms in the center of the state. Even though Indiana is relatively small, it ranks among the top ten states in both agriculture and industrial production.

Indiana is also an amazingly beautiful land. Its scenery varies from the lakefront country of the north to the bluffs and forests of the south. Millions of tourists come each year to see such marvels as the Indiana sand dunes that line Lake Michigan's shore. To visitors and to students, Hoosierland extends a hearty welcome.

Chapter 2
THE LAND

THE LAND

Round my Indiana homestead wave the cornfields.
In the distance loom the woodlands clear and cool.
Oftentimes my thoughts revert to scenes of childhood
Where I first received my lessons, nature's school.
—From the state song,
"On the Banks of the Wabash, Far Away"

GEOGRAPHY

"The Crossroads of America," the Indiana state motto, can be traced back to the early 1800s, when the east-west National Road and the north-south Michigan Road crossed in Indianapolis. Today, more major highways intersect in Indiana than in any other state. Indianapolis is a twelve-hour drive from half the population of the United States.

Indiana's total area is 36,291 square miles (93,994 square kilometers). In terms of size, it ranks thirty-eighth among the states, and is the smallest of the twelve midwestern states. Indiana is bounded by Lake Michigan and the state of Michigan on the north, Ohio on the east, Illinois on the west, and Kentucky on the south. Indianapolis is the state capital and the largest city.

LAND REGIONS

For nearly 400,000 years, the northern two-thirds of Indiana was covered and re-covered by mountains of glacial ice. The last of the glaciers retreated from midwestern America more than

The Lake Michigan shoreline at Indiana Dunes State Park

10,000 years ago. Glaciers grinding over the earth made the north a flatland, while the southern tip remained wrinkled.

In geological terms, ancient glacial activity divided Indiana into three major land regions: the Great Lakes Plains, the Till Plains area and the Southern Hills and Lowlands. The Great Lakes Plains makes up the northern quarter of the state. It is a level, moist region that harbors many lakes and ponds. A highlight of the Great Lakes Plains is the lovely Indiana sand dune area. The Till Plains area, in the state's midsection, is named after the rows of debris (or till) left by advancing and retreating glaciers. A traveler driving through the Till Plains sees some sections of land that are as flat as a calm sea and other areas that are graced with gentle hills that roll like waves. The Till Plains harbors Indiana's most fertile soil. The Southern Hills and Lowlands area is blessed with stunning scenery, but its farmland is not as rich as that of the north. Glaciers usually leave fertile soil in their wake, and this section of the state did not benefit from their passage.

A shipping barge makes the turn at the bend of the Ohio River near Leavenworth.

RIVERS AND LAKES

Heralded in songs and poems, the mighty Wabash is one of Indiana's most important rivers. In the southwest, the Wabash forms the Hoosier State border with Illinois. In the north, the Wabash snakes across the state, its distant fingers reaching the Ohio border. Major branches of the Wabash include the White, the Eel, the Mississinewa, the Salamonie, and the Tippecanoe. With its tributaries, the Wabash drains more than two-thirds of Indiana's rain and melted snow.

The Kankakee, the Pigeon, and the St. Joseph are other major rivers in the north. Most of the state's rivers flow south and west, eventually emptying into the Mississippi. In northeastern Indiana,

however, the Maumee flows north and east to drain into Lake
Erie. In the south, the broad Ohio River forms Indiana's border
with Kentucky. Some of the first American farming communities
were built along the Ohio Valley in the early 1800s.

Indiana's shoreline with Lake Michigan is only 40 miles
(64 kilometers) long, but Indiana is still considered a Great Lakes
state. From ancient times until today, the Great Lakes have had a
profound effect on Indiana's people. Northern Indiana has about
four hundred lakes. So many lakes dot the northeast that a map of
the region looks like Swiss cheese. Lake Wawasee, in the north, is
the state's largest natural lake. Other major lakes in the north
include Bass Lake, Maxinkuckee Lake, and Lake James. In central
Indiana, Mississinewa Lake, Salamonie Lake, and Huntington
Lake were created by dams built in river systems. Lakes are fewer
in southern Indiana. Monroe Lake, the largest lake in the south,
also was created by a dam.

PLANTS AND ANIMALS

Before the pioneers arrived, more than 80 percent of Indiana
was covered by forest. Thick woods stood everywhere except in
the wetlands of the northeast. Then, frontier farmers, loggers, and
raging fires took their toll. Today, only 17 percent of the state is
classified as forested. The thickest forests are found in the south,
where the marvelous Hoosier National Forest is a playground for
lovers of the outdoors.

More than one hundred species of trees are native to Indiana,
including seventeen varieties of oak. Common trees include ash,
beech, black willow, elm, maple, oak, sycamore, and tamarack.
The yellow poplar (also called the tulip tree) is the state tree. The
sand dunes region alone is home to more than three thousand

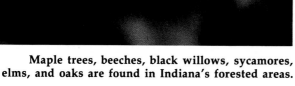
Maple trees, beeches, black willows, sycamores, elms, and oaks are found in Indiana's forested areas.

varieties of bushes and plants. Jack-in-the-pulpits and spring beauties are wildflowers that grow throughout the state. The peony is the state flower.

Herds of deer roam Indiana's forests and grasslands. The red fox is the state's most common carnivorous animal. Bobcats and badgers still live in the state, but they are rare and are considered to be endangered species. Frequently seen wild animals include cottontail rabbits, raccoons, and opossums. Waterfowl, including black ducks and great blue herons, nest in the many shining lakes of northern Indiana. The cardinal, which sings its tunes in every corner of the state, is the state bird. Catfish, bass, pike, salmon, bluegills, crappies, and sunfish are found in the state's streams and lakes.

AN UNDERGROUND TREASURE

Deep below the earth in southern Indiana is a sea of limestone. The limestone formed some 300 million years ago when the

Spring beauties grow throughout the state and great blue herons nest in northern Indiana lakes.

region was a shallow ocean bed. As tiny sea creatures died, their bones piled up and eventually hardened into the thick, smooth rock we call limestone. Today, this ancient ocean—known as the Salem Outcrop—is one of the richest deposits of top-quality limestone found anywhere on earth.

New York City's Empire State Building and Rockefeller Center are built from Indiana limestone. The stone was also used in the construction of the Pentagon, the United States Treasury, and a dozen other government buildings in Washington, D.C. Fourteen state capitols around the nation are built from this sturdy and very beautiful material.

The seabed that once covered southern Indiana also left the region with a spectacular network of limestone caves. There are more than seven hundred known limestone caves in southern Indiana. Many more caverns probably exist undiscovered below the earth. Wyandotte, Marengo, and Bluesprings are the most famous caves in the state. These underground labyrinths attract both the curious tourist and the serious cave explorer.

15

An autumn view of Hoosier National Forest and snow-covered dunes at the shore of Lake Michigan illustrate two of Indiana's four contrasting seasons.

CLIMATE

Typical of the American Midwest, Indiana has hot, often humid, summers, and chilly winters. The extreme temperatures recorded in the state reflect the differences in seasons. In February 1951, the temperature dropped to minus 35 degrees Fahrenheit (minus 37 degrees Celsius) at Greensburg, and in July 1936, the people of Collegeville sweltered through a day that saw the thermometer reach 116 degrees Fahrenheit (47 degrees Celsius).

Generally, winters are less chilly in the south than in the northern part of the state, but the temperature difference is not

16

dramatic. During January, the city of Evansville, in the south, has an average temperature of 35 degrees Fahrenheit (2 degrees Celsius), while the northern city of South Bend averages 25 degrees Fahrenheit (minus 4 degrees Celsius). Average July temperatures range from 73 degrees Fahrenheit (23 degrees Celsius) in South Bend to 78 degrees Fahrenheit (26 degrees Celsius) in Evansville. Farmers in the south enjoy a 200-day growing season, but in the north the growing season is only 150 days a year.

With no mountains to act as a buffer, strong winds and even tornadoes sometimes twist across the state. Summer storms are often accompanied by howling winds and pelting hail. Usually, though, a summer breeze is a welcome relief during sultry July and August nights.

Indiana receives about 36 inches (91 centimeters) of rainfall a year. For the most part, the south gets more rain than the north. Droughts and floods occur, but both are rare. Older residents still talk about the great Ohio River flood of 1937 that killed dozens of people and devastated entire towns. In the winter months, northern Indiana receives far more snow than does the south. On days when South Bend (near the northern border) is covered by a foot of snow, Bloomington (in the south) may receive little more than a chilling drizzle.

From border to border, Indiana is a scenic state, its land loved by all Hoosiers. The people's reverence for the land is reflected in the very haunting state song. The song is the lamentation of a wandering Hoosier, far from home, longing to see the land he loves:

> Oh, the moonlight's fair tonight along the Wabash,
> From the hills there comes the breath of new-mown hay.
> Through the sycamores the candlelights are gleaming,
> On the banks of the Wabash, far away.

Chapter 3
THE PEOPLE

THE PEOPLE

I insist that the Hoosier is different mentally
and spiritually from the average American.
He is softer, less sophisticated, more poetic. . . .
He dreams a lot. He likes to play in simple ways.
He is not as grasping as other Americans. . . .
He has the temperament of the artist.
—Theodore Dreiser, a famous writer from Indiana

POPULATION AND POPULATION DISTRIBUTION

The 1980 census gave Indiana a population of 5,490,260 people,
a gain of 5.7 percent over the 1970 population figure. The United
States as a whole gained 11.4 percent between 1970 and 1980.
Indiana's estimated 1985 population was 5,449,000. Among the
fifty states, Indiana ranks twelfth in population.

About two-thirds of all Hoosiers live in cities and towns. In
1900, the state's rural versus urban population was the reversal of
the present, with two-thirds of the people living on farms, and
only one-third making their homes in cities and towns.

Indiana does not have a single towering metropolis that
dominates cultural and economic life. Instead, the people are
gathered in several population centers scattered throughout the
state. Indianapolis, which is located at the geographical middle of
the state, is the largest population center. The second-most
populous area is located along the Lake Michigan shore and is
called northwestern Indiana, the Calumet region, or simply "the

Calumet." The cities of the Calumet (named after Illinois' Calumet River and Lake Calumet) are East Chicago, Gary, Hammond, and Whiting. Fort Wayne and its suburbs, located in the northeast, hold the state's third-largest concentration of people.

Indiana has five cities with populations greater than 100,000. In order of population, the state's largest cities are: Indianapolis (700,807), Fort Wayne (172,349), Gary (151,953), Evansville (130,496), and South Bend (109,727).

WHO ARE THE HOOSIERS?

More than 98 percent of Indiana's residents are native-born Americans. About 7 percent of the state's citizens are black. People of Hispanic heritage comprise 1 percent of the population. Asians are a small but fast-growing group. Although Indiana means "Land of the Indians," there are fewer than eight thousand Native Americans living in the state today.

Indiana was settled by three major movements of immigrants. The first wave of settlers came from the southern United States, especially Virginia, Kentucky, and the Carolinas. Those frontiersmen established farms and villages in the southern half of Indiana. The farmland in the north was settled by pioneers from New York, Pennsylvania, and New England. A third and smaller group of immigrants came directly from Europe to take industrial jobs in the smoky steel mills of Gary and the other Calumet cities.

To a certain extent, patterns set by the initial waves of settlers can be recognized today. Indiana's old Route 40, which runs through the center of the state, serves as a Hoosier Mason and Dixon's line. People living north of Route 40 tend to speak in flat midwestern accents, while a southern drawl prevails south of the highway. In the south, some people use old southern expressions

Two-thirds of the state's people live in urban areas. These Hoosiers, residents of the largest city in Indiana, are enjoying the shops and restaurants of the Indianapolis Union Station.

such as "clabber cheese" for cottage cheese and "goobers" for peanuts.

Blacks have lived in Indiana since the earliest pioneer days, but in 1910 they constituted less than 2 percent of the state's population. During the two world wars, however, thousands of blacks seeking factory jobs came to Indiana from the southern states. Today, blacks live throughout Indiana, but they are concentrated in the industrial northwest and in the Indianapolis region. Two of every three of the state's blacks live either in Gary or in the Indianapolis area.

RELIGION

Roman Catholicism is the oldest Christian faith practiced in Indiana. French fur traders brought the Catholic religion to Indiana more than two hundred years ago. Today, Roman Catholics make up the state's largest church group. The Methodist church is the largest Protestant denomination, followed by the United Church of Christ, Baptist, Lutheran, and Presbyterian churches. The Jewish population of Indiana is about 22,000.

These boys on their way to school are members of the large Amish community of northeastern Indiana.

Many Mennonite and Amish people live in the farmland of northeastern Indiana. The first Mennonite church, at Berne, has one of the largest Mennonite congregations in the United States. The Mennonites originated in Switzerland in the 1500s. In their interpretation, the Bible forbids them to go to war or to swear oaths of allegiance to man-made institutions. The Amish are an offshoot of the Mennonite religion. Generations ago, Amish families established farms in Pennsylvania, Ohio, and Indiana. According to Amish *ordnung* (rules), sect members are forbidden to drive cars, use electricity, or go to public places of entertainment. Horse-drawn buggies driven by black-clad Amish men and women are a common sight in the rural northeast.

POLITICS

Around the nation, Indiana is thought of as a conservative, Republican state. Indeed, voting patterns confirm Republican leanings. Even in the early 1980s, when the economic recession closed factories and sent unemployment soaring, the Republicans maintained power. From 1940 to 1988, Hoosiers gave the majority of their votes to the Republican presidential candidate in every election but one. The lone exception was 1964, when Lyndon Johnson carried the state. Indiana's most influential newspaper is the conservative, pro-Republican Indianapolis *Star*, owned by the powerful Pulliam family. Republican Dan Quayle, a grandson of Eugene Pulliam, served as a United States senator until he was elected vice-president in 1988. Another conservative influence on state politics is the American Legion, which was founded in Indiana.

Yet it is a mistake to think that all Hoosiers are Republican loyalists. Studies show that in any given election, as many as 300,000 Indiana voters split their ballots and cross parties. In the 1960s and 1970s, Indiana was represented in the United States Senate by Vance Hartke and Birch Bayh—two liberal Democrats. The 1988 election serves as an example of the independence of Indiana's voters. In 1988, Republican presidential nominee George Bush, with Dan Quayle as his running mate, carried the state in a landslide, and Republican senator Richard Lugar won reelection with a record 760,000 votes. But in that same election, voters chose Democrat Evan Bayh (the son of Birch Bayh) as their governor. When Evan Bayh took office in 1989, he became the state's first Democratic governor in twenty years.

Through the years, Indiana has been home to colorful politicians and to powerful political machines. Until recently, state employees were required to "contribute" 2 percent of their wages to the political party in power. Armed with those funds, party organizations grew mighty. Famous Indiana political figures include William Jenner, who served in the United States Senate after World War II and was so anti-Communist that he once called army hero General George Marshall "a front man for traitors." On the opposite extreme was labor leader Eugene Debs, who early in the century ran for president five times as a Socialist.

Chapter 4
THE BEGINNING

THE BEGINNING

*My heart is a stone: heavy with sadness for my people,
cold with the knowledge that no treaty will keep the whites
out of our lands. . . . But hear me: a single twig breaks,
but the bundle of twigs is strong. Some day I will
embrace our brother tribes and draw them into a bundle,
and together we will win our country back.*
—Tecumseh, a Shawnee chief

THE FIRST RESIDENTS

More than ten thousand years ago, wandering bands of hunters first stepped upon the land we now call Indiana. The hunters were part of a great wave of men and women who crossed Bering Sea land bridges and trekked from Asia to North America. Thousands of years later, Europeans called those original Americans "Indians."

The first human inhabitants of the Great Lakes region may have hunted now-extinct animals such as mammoths and mastodons. When those animals disappeared, the hunters turned to deer, elk, and bison. Spear points belonging to prehistoric people have been found in Indiana and other parts of the Midwest. In several Indiana sites, archaeologists have uncovered ancient garbage heaps composed of animal bones and huge piles of clam shells.

About 1000 B.C., the people of the upper Midwest developed farming and began to depend less on hunting. An agricultural economy enabled them to establish permanent villages and indulge in the arts. Craft workers of the time made beautifully decorated pottery, finely carved stone figures of animals and human beings, and sparkling jewelry. Farming also fostered a mound-building civilization that flourished in Indiana and neighboring states.

Mound building began along the banks of the Ohio River around 600 B.C. For reasons that are lost to history, small armies of workers built earthen structures in the shape of pyramids, cones, or sacred circles. Early woodland cultures used their creations as burial sites; later peoples built mounds as centers of worship.

At least one-third of all present-day Indiana counties contain remains of mounds built long ago. The most famous group of Indiana mounds is at Mounds State Park, near the town of Anderson. At the park stand eleven ancient earthworks, the largest of which measures 360 feet (110 meters) in diameter. Angel Mounds, at the Ohio River city of Evansville, is another legacy of the Indian cultures. Archaeologists estimate that Angel Mounds was the center of a village that once held a thousand people.

In the early 1700s, when French fur traders arrived, the tribes of Indiana were in a state of confusing transition. Indian wars in the East, which were sparked by the European fur trade, disrupted American Indian society and spurred great movements of tribes. Groups such as the Miamis and their relatives, the Weas, the Potawatomis, the Kickapoos, and the Piankashaws were recent arrivals in Indiana. The Delawares, Munsees, and Shawnees lived along the Atlantic seaboard until bloody wars drove them west to the Ohio Valley. Life in the Indiana region was in such a state of flux in the 1700s that most tribes stayed in the area for only twenty-five to fifty years before migrating farther west.

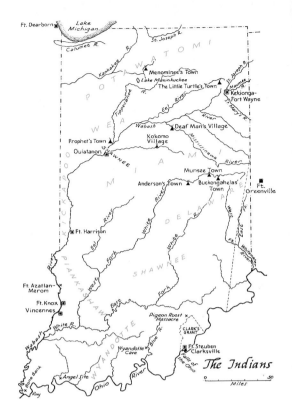

A figurine found at Angel Mounds (above) shows the artistic skill of the early people who inhabited a large village at the site.

The map on the left shows the general location of the Indian groups living in Indiana during the 1700s and early 1800s.

Of all the peoples who passed through Indiana, the Miamis established the most permanent roots, remaining in the state for almost 150 years. The Miamis settled in central and northern Indiana, occupying a territory that extended from the middle Wabash to what is now Fort Wayne. They lived in villages where they planted corn, beans, and pumpkins. Their houses consisted of poles stuck in the ground and covered with bark or cattail mats. Patches of deerskin intricately sewn together served as clothing. Music and dance filled their villages during festive times. Their instruments consisted of drums made from animal skins and rattles fashioned from gourds. The Miamis were a sternly religious people who believed in an all-powerful creator, a host of lesser gods, and a life after death. To them, good and evil spirits lurked everywhere—in the forests, in the rivers, and even inside solid rocks.

French fur traders, called *voyageurs*, used sturdy canoes to transport pelts to the forts along Indiana's rivers.

THE FRENCH AND THE BRITISH

The first European known to have visited Indiana was French explorer René-Robert Cavelier, Sieur de La Salle, who passed through the region in 1679. La Salle was a representative of New France, a nation based in Canada and one whose leaders claimed most of midwestern America.

In 1681, La Salle made a second journey around the curve in the St. Joseph River, where South Bend stands today. Under the shade of a broad oak tree, he met with the chiefs of the Miamis and their neighbors, the Illinois. He tried to persuade the two groups to unite and stand against the Iroquois, the powerful eastern Indians who were allies of the British. La Salle's efforts at diplomacy were unsuccessful, but a witness to the talks still survives. At South Bend's Highland Cemetery stands the Council Oak Tree, believed to be the same tree that shaded the meeting between La Salle and the tribal chiefs more than three hundred years ago.

After La Salle and others explored the Great Lakes region, French leaders claimed the land for New France. Since rivers served as highways, French authorities built a series of forts along strategic riverbanks. The forts regulated the very profitable fur trade, and prevented the British from moving into territory claimed by New France. In Indiana, three riverside forts rose during the 1700s: Fort Ouiatenon, just south of the present-day city of Lafayette; Fort Miami, at the site of modern-day Fort Wayne; and Fort Vincennes, at today's city of Vincennes. These three forts were the first permanent white settlements in Indiana.

Outside the log walls of the forts, tiny villages developed. Village life was French in character, but the Europeans' numbers were small. In 1746, Vincennes reported a population of 750 Indians, 20 Frenchmen, and 5 blacks. The villages were lawless places where brawls and shootings were common. Fur trading was a seasonal occupation, and the men had too much time on their hands. As one traveler wrote, "The French inhabitants of Vincennes are an idle, lazy people, a parcel of French renegades. . . ."

Many of the French married Indians. Some important figures of early Indiana history were of mixed French and Indian blood. One was Zachariah Cicot, son of a French father and a Potawatomi mother. Cicot served as a scout for American army leaders, and later founded the town of Independence. Francis Godfroy, who was also half French and half Indian, became a Miami chief and led the tribe on its last war party. Eventually, Godfroy opened a trading post near the town of Peru and grew wealthy.

The most dedicated of the Frenchmen in the New World were the Catholic priests who risked their lives to preach Christianity

St. Francis Xavier Cathedral (left) was built on the site of the first log chapel built in Vincennes, in 1732.

Francis Godfroy, the last of the Miami chiefs (above), eventually opened a trading post near the town of Peru.

to the Indians. Members of the Jesuit order of priests usually led the way into the wilderness of New France. Many historians believe that Jesuit Father Jacques Marquette landed on Indiana's shores even before La Salle. The first Christian church in Indiana rose at Vincennes in 1732. Father Xavier de Givinne, a Jesuit, was its earliest priest.

Although they had few settlers in the region, French presence in Indiana lasted almost one hundred years. Finally, the centuries-old rivalry between England and France exploded into the French and Indian War. The British won the war, and upon signing the Treaty of Paris in 1763, the French surrendered their claims to the lower Great Lakes region. For Indiana, a new historical chapter began.

To the Indians, the shift in power from the French to the British was a calamity. Aloof and arrogant, the British refused to commingle with the Indians as the French had done for decades. The Indians, who had regarded the French as brothers, looked upon the British as rulers. Under the leadership of Ottawa chief Pontiac, an alliance of Indian tribes attacked the Great Lakes forts soon after the British took command. In the Indiana region, Fort Ouiatenon and Fort Miami fell before the Indian onslaught: Pontiac's rebellion failed, however, because his warriors were unable to conquer the vital Great Lakes fort at Detroit.

THE AMERICANS

Far to the east of Indiana, beyond the Appalachian Mountains, spread the thirteen British colonies. Living on the fringes of the colonies were inveterate pioneers who hungered to settle the untouched land that lay just over the next mountaintop, or was "just a piece" farther down the river. It was often joked that these American families felt crowded as soon as they could see their neighbors' chimney smoke.

In the 1770s, tiny bands of Americans began rafting down the Ohio River to stake out farms in Ohio and Kentucky. British law forbade settlement beyond the Appalachian Mountains, but defying the British was becoming an accepted practice in the American colonies.

The French and Indian War had emptied the British treasury. To recoup their war losses, the British imposed taxes on tea and other items used by the colonies. Anger over the taxes led to the Revolutionary War and the birth of a new nation.

The Revolutionary War produced many American heroes, but in the minds of Indianans, none is more honored than George Rogers Clark. Born in Virginia, Clark spent his youth in the backwoods of Kentucky, where he became an accomplished hunter and trailblazer. Soon after the Revolutionary War began, Clark and a party of 175 men trekked across the western forests and captured British Fort Kaskaskia in present-day Illinois. At Kaskaskia, Clark persuaded Jesuit priest Pierre Gibault to travel to Vincennes and rally the French settlers there to the American cause.

In Fort Detroit, British governor Henry Hamilton fumed over the loss of Kaskaskia and Vincennes. The governor was so zealous in encouraging Indian war parties to take American scalps that he earned a loathsome nickname — Hair Buyer Hamilton. Leading an army of six hundred men, Hamilton marched south and recaptured Fort Sackville, near Vincennes, in December 1778. With winter closing in, Hamilton believed he was safe from counterattack and dismissed all but eighty of his soldiers. But Vincennes resident Francis Vigo, an Italian-born merchant who was sympathetic to the Americans, raced his canoe to Kaskaskia and told George Rogers Clark that Fort Sackville was poorly defended. Clark decided to attack, and his boldness helped the Americans win the Revolutionary War.

In the bitter January of 1779, Clark led his tiny army on a 240-mile (386-kilometer) march through hip-deep fields of snow and over icy streams and swamps. Upon arriving at the outskirts of Vincennes, Clark and his men were secretly resupplied by pro-American townspeople. Clark surrounded Fort Sackville at night, and when dawn broke, his Kentucky sharpshooters blazed away at the red-coated defenders. The astonished British were forced to surrender.

At the end of the war, the British ceded to the United States a huge territory composed of present-day Ohio, Indiana, Illinois, Wisconsin, and parts of Minnesota. Most of this land, which was called the Northwest Territory, was completely devoid of

In the winter of 1779, George Rogers Clark's band of French and American volunteers slogged through icy streams and swamps during a seventeen-day march to capture the British-held fort at Vincennes.

American settlers. To govern the region, Congress passed the remarkable Northwest Ordinance. Provisions in the ordinance forbade slavery in the Northwest Territory, guaranteed freedom of religion to all settlers, and laid the ground rules for forming new states from regions in the territory. Most important, the Northwest Ordinance held that new states, once accepted into the American Union, would have all the rights and privileges of the established states.

THE LAST INDIAN WARS

Within a year of the passage of the Northwest Ordinance, some twenty thousand American settlers rafted down the Ohio River seeking new farmland. To the frontier farmers, the open lands represented the fulfillment of the American dream. To the Indians, the army of pioneers was an invasion.

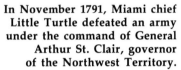
In November 1791, Miami chief Little Turtle defeated an army under the command of General Arthur St. Clair, governor of the Northwest Territory.

Boldest of the Indian leaders in the Northwest Territory was Miami chief Little Turtle. Born near present-day Fort Wayne, Little Turtle had an uncanny military mind. In battle, he combined tactics used by white generals with the Indians' ability to fight in the wilderness. In 1790, Little Turtle lured an army led by General Josiah Harmar into the Maumee River Valley, where he unleashed a surprise attack, routing the Americans. A year later, in a battle fought near today's city of Portland, Little Turtle defeated an army under the command of General Arthur St. Clair, governor of the Northwest Territory. St. Clair lost 630 men of his 3,000-man force, making it the most costly defeat suffered by the United States Army at the hands of Indians.

Frustrated by the constant setbacks, President George Washington chose General Anthony Wayne to take charge in the Northwest Territory. During the Revolutionary War, the general was called "Mad Anthony" Wayne because of his daring exploits in battle. Wayne drilled his troops relentlessly, and never failed to post guards around his camp to prevent surprise attacks. Speaking

After the Battle of Fallen Timbers, General Anthony Wayne built Fort Wayne on the site of a Miami village. The site eventually became Indiana's second-largest city, and the reconstructed fort (left) is now a tourist attraction.

of his enemy, Little Turtle remarked, "The Americans are now led by a chief who never sleeps." At the Battle of Fallen Timbers, fought in 1794 near present-day Toledo, Ohio, Wayne's men crushed the Miamis and other tribes. After the battle, the American general marched into Indiana and built Fort Wayne at the confluence of the St. Marys and St. Joseph rivers. That crude wilderness fort, built over the site of a Miami village, eventually became Indiana's second-largest city.

The Indian wars did not end with the Battle of Fallen Timbers. As the War of 1812 approached, the British encouraged Great Lakes Indians to attack American settlements in the Northwest Territory. Once again, the region felt the fury of gun and tomahawk.

At the forefront of the new conflict was Shawnee leader Tecumseh. A passionate speaker and tireless political organizer,

On November 7, 1811, at the Battle of Tippecanoe, American troops led by General William Henry Harrison defeated an alliance of Indians led by the Shawnee leader called the Prophet.

Tecumseh persuaded Great Lakes Indians to put aside their tribal jealousies and unite against the white enemy. A white man who listened to one of Tecumseh's fiery speeches reported, "His eyes burned with supernatural luster, and his whole frame trembled with emotion. His voice resounded . . . like a succession of thunderbolts."

Tecumseh and his brother, known as the Prophet, founded a religious community along the banks of the Tippecanoe River near present-day Lafayette. Fearing Indian rebellion, General William Henry Harrison, governor of the newly formed Indiana Territory, gathered an army and marched toward the village. Tecumseh was away from the village at the time, and his brother rallied the warriors by telling them that his magic would lead the way to victory. The Prophet claimed that the gods would make the Indians invisible and that the soldiers' bullets would be as soft

At Tippecanoe Battlefield, actors dressed in 1811 U.S. infantry costumes reenact the battle.
A monument with General William Henry Harrison's statue marks the site of the army encampment.

as rainwater. At the Battle of Tippecanoe, fought in November 1811 just north of Lafayette, the Indians charged into Harrison's camp with such astonishing courage that the troops fell back. But the ranks stiffened, and Harrison's superior firepower cut down the Indian attackers. The defeat destroyed Tecumseh's dream of uniting all Indian tribes to resist white expansion.

For William Henry Harrison, Tippecanoe was both a military and a political victory. Thirty years later, Harrison (with John Tyler as his running mate) campaigned for president under the slogan, "Tippecanoe and Tyler too." Harrison won the election and became the ninth president of the United States.

Other skirmishes followed the Tippecanoe battle, but Indian resistance had lost its thrust. During the coming decades, the proud, original residents of the state were forced to flee west, leaving behind them mounds and memories, blood and tears.

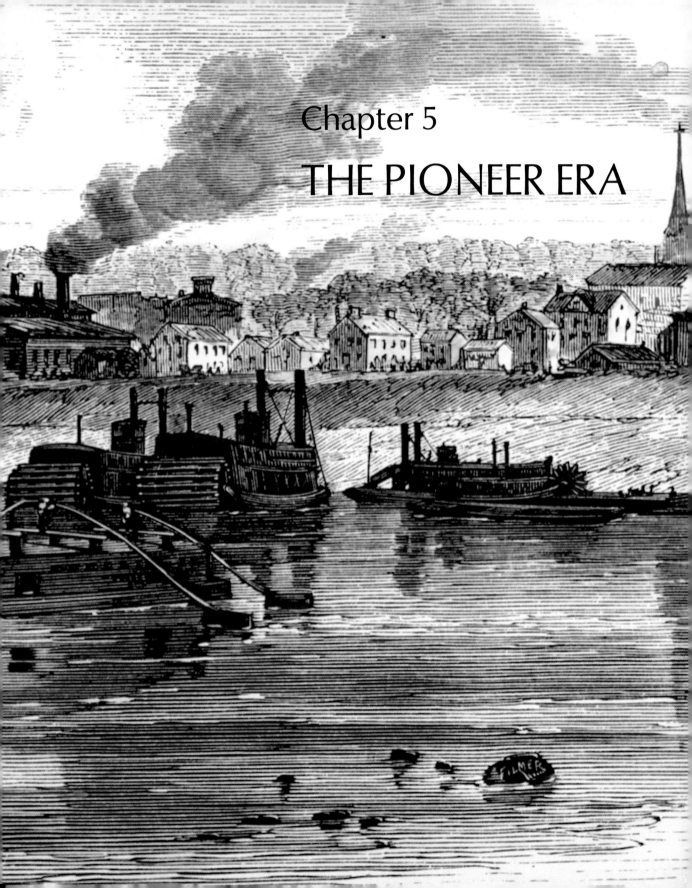

Chapter 5

THE PIONEER ERA

THE PIONEER ERA

No soil produces a greater abundance than that of Indiana.
—From a frontier newspaper, the *Indiana Gazette*

STATEHOOD

By 1815, more than sixty thousand pioneers lived in the
territory called Indiana. After its boundaries were fixed by
Congress, Indiana was eligible to become a state. Resident voters
drafted a constitution, and on December 11, 1816, Indiana was
officially accepted as the nineteenth state to enter the American
Union. A lawyer named Jonathan Jennings was elected the first
governor. The first capital was at the southern Indiana town of
Corydon. In 1820, government leaders chose an undeveloped site
in the central part of the state to serve as a capital city. The new
city was called Indianapolis, although many legislators wanted to
name it Tecumseh.

Statehood launched the pioneer era in Indiana history. It was an
exciting period that saw thousands of settlers arrive full of hope,
but prepared for toil and sacrifice.

COMMUNITIES ON THE FRONTIER

River ports in the south were the state's busiest towns. The first
settlers of the Ohio River town of Madison (named in 1809 for
President James Madison) arrived in 1805. By 1830, Madison held

Surveyor Alexander Ralston designed the capital city of Indianapolis with four major diagonal streets leading to a city center dominated by government buildings.

two thousand people and was Indiana's most populous city. Farther east on the Ohio River was New Albany, founded in 1813. New Albany became a bustling shipbuilding center, and its shipyards launched many splendid riverboats. Evansville began in 1812 when a Revolutionary War veteran named Hugh McGary built a cabin on what is today Main Street.

While most Indiana settlements grew haphazardly, Indianapolis was a planned city from the beginning. The capital grew from a design developed by surveyor Alexander Ralston, who had worked with Pierre L'Enfant, the city planner of Washington, D.C. Ralston laid out Indianapolis with four major diagonal streets leading to a city center to be dominated by government buildings.

The community of New Harmony as it looked in 1832

Religious communities were common on the Indiana frontier. Societies of Quakers sprouted up in and around Richmond in the east-central part of the state. The Shakers founded a community near Oaktown in 1804. They were called Shakers because the intense emotions generated during worship caused their bodies to shiver and shake. Black farmers who settled near Carthage in pioneeer times formed a religious community centered on the African Methodist Episcopal church. Of all frontier communities, none had a history so rich as the Wabash River town of New Harmony and its earlier incarnation, Harmonie.

As the night watchman made his rounds on the streets of Harmonie, he cried a mournful verse: "Again a day is past and a step made nearer to our end. Our time runs away and the joys of heaven are our reward." Harmonie was founded by religious

Thrall's Opera House in New Harmony, built about 1824, was originally used as a community house.

leader George Rapp, who brought a group of eight hundred German immigrants to the Wabash River site in 1815. Rapp believed the world would soon end, and he hoped to prepare his followers for Judgment Day. The people laid out streets, built houses, and cleared farmland. But instead of meeting its doom, the farming community thrived. The group was so successful that Rapp feared his followers would become corrupted by money and materialism. In 1824, Rapp sold his holdings in Harmonie to a wealthy British idealist named Robert Owen, who launched a second experiment in living at the site.

Owen dreamed of establishing a socialistic community in which property and income would be shared equally among all residents. About a thousand followers of Owen, called Owenites, moved in and renamed the city New Harmony. Trouble brewed at the very start of New Harmony society. Some Owenites were self-styled intellectuals who thought that only their ideas and their plans should prevail. Still other Owenites were lazy and tried to live off the labor of their fellows. Community members fell into endless bickering while weeds grew in the fields and workshops

The boyhood home of Abraham Lincoln, at Lincoln Boyhood National Memorial, has been restored. The Lincolns, like most Indiana pioneers, lived in a one-room log cabin.

were left unattended. The experimental community at New Harmony failed, but the town remained Indiana's leading intellectual and artistic center throughout the pioneer era.

LIFE ON PIONEER FARMS

The first great wave of farmers came from the southern states, mainly Kentucky, Virginia, and the Carolinas. The settlers occupied the southern half of the state first, buying land from the federal government at low prices. Most farm families arriving in Indiana were veteran pioneers, accustomed to carving farms out of forests. A typical family was that headed by Thomas and Nancy Lincoln, who walked from Kentucky to Spencer County, Indiana, in 1816. Traveling with the Lincolns was their son, seven-year-old Abraham. The boy who was to become one of the greatest presidents in American history lived in Indiana for the next fourteen years, until he was twenty-one and moved to Illinois.

Most Indiana pioneers lived in crudely built log cabins about the size of a modern two-car garage. Large families were typical on the Indiana frontier, and individual privacy was nonexistent in the tiny cabins that usually held as many as ten noisy children.

Corn was the staple crop in early Indiana. Frontier families ate corn three times a day, either as mush or as a side dish in the form of corn pone (corn bread). Frontiersmen were hunters as well as farmers. Wild turkey and deer meat were main courses at meals. When game became scarce, Indiana families relied on hogs for meat. Women, assisted by their children, tended gardens where they grew potatoes, squash, cabbage, and other vegetables. The planting of flowers was a sign of prosperity in log-cabin days.

Providing for schools was a challenge for Indiana pioneer communities. The state constitution of 1816 directed the legislature to establish and maintain tax-supported schools free of charge for all residents. At the time, Indiana had the only state constitution that required the government to provide public schools. But the few tax dollars collected by the state during pioneer times were usually spent for building roads and draining marshlands. It was not until the 1850s that state government was able to establish a public school system. In the meantime, farming families pitched in to build log schoolhouses, and each student paid a few dollars toward the teachers' salaries. Since many adults had not learned to read or write, it was common to see a thirty-year-old mother or father sitting in the same classroom with ten-year-old children.

Epidemic diseases were the greatest danger faced by pioneer families. Cholera epidemics struck down hundreds of Indiana pioneers during 1833 and 1849. A disease called milk sickness, which killed Nancy Lincoln, scourged many communities. Doctors were few on the Indiana frontier. It was usually the job of

Hanover College, founded in 1827, is the oldest private college in Indiana. This photograph of one of the campus buildings was taken in 1897.

the pioneer mother to nurse her children through flu and fever as best she could. Folk remedies to correct or prevent sicknesses abounded: a toad held over a rattlesnake bite was said to draw off the poison; onions carried in the pocket were believed to prevent snakebite; a dead spider worn around the neck was thought to ward off a host of diseases.

Struggling frontier families found strength and joy in religion. New communities were served by circuit-riding preachers who used their wagons as pulpits and held services in cornfields. Circuit-riding preachers were famous for their fire-and-brimstone sermons. They thundered out warnings to obey God and reject sin. Working together, farming communities soon constructed log churches and meetinghouses.

Church organizations were the first institutions to support higher education in Indiana. In 1827, the Presbyterians established

The National Road became the main road for pioneers traveling to
Indiana from the East and contributed to the state's rapid growth.

Hanover College, near Madison; and five years later, a
Presbyterian group built Wabash College in Crawfordsville. The
Methodists founded Asbury College (now DePauw University) at
Greencastle, in 1837. Earlham College, at Richmond, was a Quaker
school started in 1847. That same year, the first Catholic college in
the state—the now-famous University of Notre Dame—was
established far to the north, in South Bend.

SETTLEMENT PATTERNS AND PIONEER POLITICS

In the first forty-four years after statehood, Indiana's population
zoomed from about sixty thousand to more than one million. The
1860 census ranked Indiana as the sixth-most populous state in
the nation. Improved transportation contributed to this
spectacular growth.

Pioneer Indiana was served by two major roads and a vast
network of wagon paths. The federal government financed the

47

The ill-fated Whitewater Canal was made obsolete by the Whitewater Valley Railroad, which was built on a parallel route. The portion of the canal at Metamora, and the 1838 town itself, have been restored and are now tourist attractions.

building of the National Road, which ran from Cumberland, Maryland, to Vandalia, Illinois. The Indiana portion of the National Road (now U.S. 40) was finished in 1834. It linked Richmond, Centerville, Indianapolis, and Terre Haute. At one time, twelve different stagecoach lines ran through Indiana on the National Road. The major north-south highway was the state-funded Michigan Road, which stretched from Madison to Indianapolis, to Logansport, to South Bend, and finally to Michigan City. These roads carried heavy wagon traffic, but they were riddled with ruts and other hazards. Wrecked wagons, discarded on roadsides, were common sights.

In the 1830s, canals were dug linking the Great Lakes to Indiana's river systems. One canal-building crew was bossed by a man named Samuel Hoosier, and many historians believe the Hoosier nickname is derived from him. The canals proved to be a financial disaster for their builders and for the state. Railroads made the canal system obsolete even before its completion. Indiana's first major railroad line, linking Madison and Indianapolis, was completed in 1847. The mid-1850s saw railroad tracks stretch from New Albany to the banks of Lake Michigan. With labor in short supply, canal and railroad construction companies looked for help from out of state. Many railroad and

Indiana's first railroad, between Madison and Indianapolis, later became the Jeffersonville, Madison, & Indianapolis Railroad.

canal workers came to Indiana from Ireland. By 1850, Irish people made up 23 percent of the state's foreign-born population.

Improved transportation encouraged a second wave of migration to the Hoosier State. Traveling on railroads and canal boats, settlers from New York, Pennsylvania, and the New England states poured into relatively uncrowded northern Indiana. Farmers who worked the Till Plains discovered that its glacial soil was even richer than the soil of southern Indiana.

As the Civil War approached, political opinion drifted into two dangerously opposite camps. Newcomers in northern Indiana, as well as the state's many Quaker groups, were pro-Union and vehemently antislavery. In the southern half of the state, the old-time pioneers defended the right of southerners to own slaves.

The Hoosier attitude toward escaped slaves illustrates the divisions in the state. The farming community of Fountain City, in Wayne County, was known as the "Grand Central Station of the Underground Railroad." Members of the loose-knit Underground Railroad allowed escaped slaves to hide in their farmhouses for a day or two as they made their way north to Canada and freedom. Living in Fountain City were Levi and Katie Coffin, dedicated

49

Among the two hundred thousand Hoosiers who fought in the Civil War were these soldiers of the Fourteenth Indiana Regiment (above) and General Ambrose Burnside (right), who commanded troops in the Army of the Potomac.

Quakers and famous agents on the Underground Railroad. The Coffins estimated that they provided overnight lodging for more than two thousand runaway slaves in the years prior to the Civil War. Today, the Coffins are regarded as heroes, but pro-southern Hoosiers in the 1850s thought of them as lawbreakers. The state constitution of 1850, which was written largely by the pioneers of southern Indiana, made it illegal to assist an escaped slave. The constitution also contained a clause that forbade blacks from settling in Indiana.

When the Civil War began, however, the great majority of Indiana citizens swung their support behind a former Hoosier, President Abraham Lincoln. When Lincoln first asked for volunteers, ten thousand Hoosiers answered the call. All told, two hundred thousand Indiana citizens joined the Union ranks. Only New York contributed more men to the Union cause. Thousands of those Hoosier soldiers were wounded in battle. Some twenty-

Washington Street, Indianapolis, at Dusk, **a painting by Theodore Groll**

five thousand were killed. The bloody Civil War cost Indiana more lives than any conflict, including World War II.

Leading the state through the Civil War years was energetic governor Oliver P. Morton. A passionate supporter of Abraham Lincoln, Morton often imprisoned pro-southern sympathizers within the state. Another vigorously pro-Union Hoosier politician was former governor and powerful senator Henry S. Lane. The only fighting on Indiana soil took place in 1863, when a Confederate cavalry unit crossed the Ohio River and raided the southern Indiana towns of Corydon, Salem, Dupont, and Versailles.

For Indiana, the conclusion of the Civil War marked the end of one historical epoch and the beginning of another. The state was fully settled by the late 1860s. The pioneer era—with its hope and boundless energy—came to a close. But already the state had developed infant industries, and a new age was about to begin.

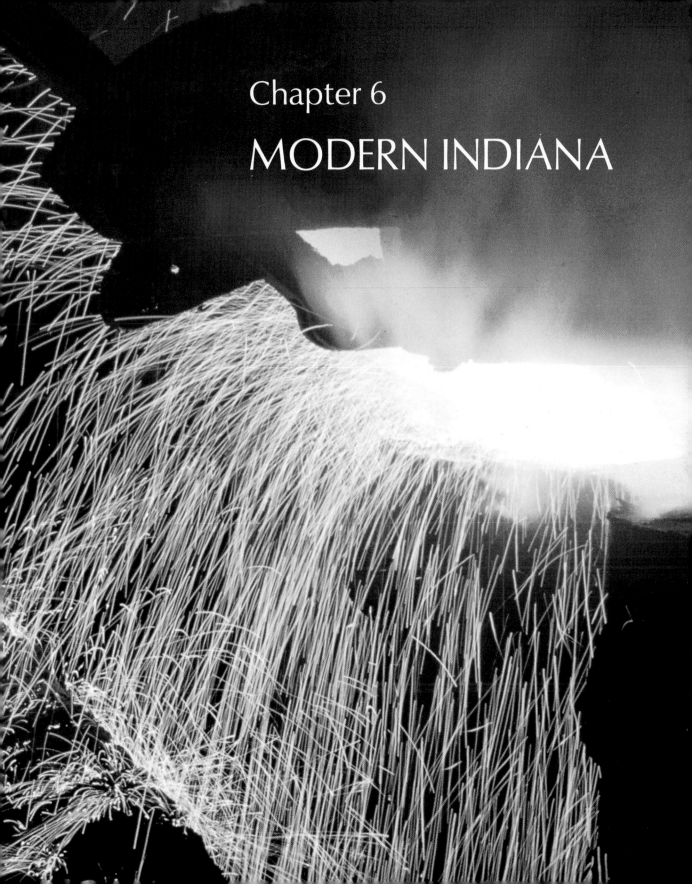

Chapter 6
MODERN INDIANA

MODERN INDIANA

This is my Indiana . . . the heartland of America,
with its pride, its prejudices, its passions.
Here are proud people with the fire of protest
in their hearts. I love it. I never had it so good.
—Irving Leibowitz, from the 1964 book *My Indiana*

INDUSTRIES AND ENTERPRISES

In the California goldfields, young John Studebaker made
wheelbarrows, which he sold to miners. Upon arriving home in
South Bend, Studebaker joined his brother Clement in the family's
blacksmith and wagon-making shop. The Studebaker Company of
South Bend soon became the nation's largest producer of horse-
drawn wagons, and years later it developed into a multimillion-
dollar automobile manufacturer.

In the post-Civil War years, other Indiana businesses succeeded
due to the inventiveness and fresh ideas of their Hoosier owners.
James Oliver, of South Bend, developed and sold a hardened steel
plow that was far more efficient than older models. In Fort
Wayne, Sylvanus F. Bowser designed the world's first practical
gasoline pump and set up a company to manufacture the device.
An Indianapolis grocer named Gilbert Van Camp discovered that
his customers enjoyed an old family recipe for pork and beans in
tomato sauce. The grocer opened up a canning company, and Van
Camp's Pork & Beans became an American staple.

Two of Indiana's most successful post-Civil War businesses were the Ball Corporation, which manufactured glass canning jars, and the Van Camp Packing Company, one of the country's major wholesale grocery suppliers.

Natural gas was discovered in east-central Indiana during the 1880s, and the find led to an industrial building boom. Towns along the "gas belt" lured factories by offering free gas and cheap land. Industries that required great sources of heat, such as glassworks, built factory complexes in Atlanta, Eaton, Elwood, Gas City, Kokomo, Middletown, Montpelier, and Portland. By the late 1800s, Indiana had 110 glassmaking plants, and ranked second in the nation in the production of glass goods. But Indiana's supply of natural gas was not as large as originally estimated, and the gas boom lasted only fifteen years.

In Muncie, however, a glassworks company started by the Ball family had a long-term impact on the town. When the gas reserves ran out, the company simply switched to coal as a source of heat. Coal was readily available from the rich mines of Terre Haute. Jars and other glass products made in Muncie were shipped to every corner of the world. Muncie's Ball State University was built mostly from funds contributed by the company's founders.

James D. ''Blue Jeans'' Williams (center) was governor of Indiana from 1877 to 1880.

Aside from industry, politics was the state's liveliest enterprise. A colorful figure of the time was Democrat James D. ''Blue Jeans'' Williams, who served as governor from 1877 to 1880. Williams championed the state's farmers, and even when working in his Indianapolis office, he wore faded blue overalls like those worn by field hands. Another prominent Hoosier political leader was Benjamin Harrison, who was born in Ohio but settled in Indianapolis as a young man. He was a grandson of William Henry Harrison, hero of the Tippecanoe battle and ninth president of the United States. In 1888, Benjamin Harrison was elected the nation's twenty-third president, the only Hoosier ever to win that office.

Two Hoosiers—Schuyler Colfax and Thomas Hendricks—served as vice-president during the late 1800s. Colfax, a newspaper editor from South Bend, was vice-president under Ulysses S. Grant. Thomas Hendricks, a Democrat from Shelbyville,

Benjamin Harrison, the twenty-third president of the United States, lived in this Indianapolis house, which has been restored with his furnishings.

was one of the most famous political leaders of his day. Hendricks served Indiana as a United States representative, United States senator, governor, and vice-president under Grover Cleveland.

PROGRESS AS A STATE

Beginning at the turn of the century, the Republican party gained great strength in Indiana. One distinguished Republican senator was Albert J. Beveridge, an eloquent speaker and a powerful writer. As a boy, Beveridge was desperately poor and worked in a railroad labor gang. Perhaps because of his bitter boyhood experiences, Beveridge led the fight to write laws banning child labor. Two more Indiana political leaders served as vice-president during the early 1900s: Charles Fairbanks, under Theodore Roosevelt, and Thomas Marshall, under Woodrow

Madame C. J. Walker, shown here at the wheel of her car in 1910, became one of the nation's first woman millionaires.

Wilson. Marshall, from Columbia City, made the famous statement, "What this country needs is a good five-cent cigar."

Small and midsized businesses made steady gains in the early 1900s. Elwood Haynes, an engineering genius who grew up in Portland, produced cars that were years ahead of their time. Working out of a factory in Kokomo, Haynes marketed the first automobile that was clutch driven and had an electrical starting system. Another midsized firm was headed by Sarah Walker, a black woman who called herself Madame C. J. Walker. She built a factory in Indianapolis to produce perfumes and other cosmetics. Walker became one of the nation's first self-made woman millionaires.

The automobile manufacturing industry had a brief but exciting fling in Indiana. From 1900 to 1920, more than two hundred different makes of cars were produced in the Hoosier State. Some of these—Duesenbergs, Auburns, Stutzes, and Maxwells—are prized antiques today. Eventually, the huge plants in Detroit overwhelmed Indiana car producers, and only Studebaker lasted beyond World War II.

This 1912 Auburn Salon (left) is one of the classic automobiles manufactured in Indiana between 1900 and 1920. In 1908, members of the Studebaker family posed in cars built in their South Bend plant (below).

Engineering genius Elwood Haynes built his first gasoline-powered automobile in 1894 (left). The following year, Haynes began to manufacture cars in a Kokomo factory.

Standard Oil built this huge refinery at Whiting in 1889.

The state's most dramatic business expansion took place in
northwest Indiana, where an empty marshland was turned into
one of the world's greatest industrial centers. Standard Oil led the
way in 1889, when the company built a huge refinery at the tiny
lakefront town of Whiting. Soon afterward, Inland Steel
constructed an open-hearth furnace complex at East Chicago. The
cities of the Calumet were logical places for the growth of heavy
industry because they lay near the large labor force in Chicago,
and their lakefront locations meant they could be served by cargo-
carrying ships. Still, few people expected the dynamic growth that
came.

Northwest Indiana's destiny as an industrial giant was sealed in
1906, when the U.S. Steel Company purchased 9,000 acres (3,642
hectares) of lakefront land and began to build the world's largest

Iron being poured at the U.S. Steel Gary works in 1914

steel-making facility. A new city, planned to accommodate 100,000 people, was laid out near the U.S. Steel plant. The city was called Gary in honor of Judge Elbert Gary, chairman of U.S. Steel. Just fifteen years after its birth, Gary was Indiana's sixth-largest city. Gary was never a pretty town. Its residents lived, worked, played, and went to school under an almost constant cloud of soot and smoke that billowed out of the steel factories. On windless days, the pollution turned high noon into gloomy dusk.

Industry fed upon industry in northwest Indiana as dozens of small factories opened to service the larger ones. Port facilities expanded. One of the nation's largest cement plants was constructed. The industrial explosion in northwest Indiana spurred the state's last major period of immigration. This time, many of the newcomers came directly from Poland, Italy,

Socialist union organizer Eugene Debs, a staunch opponent of America's entry into World War I, giving one of his many antiwar speeches in 1918

Czechoslovakia, Hungary, and other eastern and southern European countries to the Gary steel mills. Soon, half the population of Gary was foreign-born

By 1910, Indiana had almost 200,000 factory workers, a tenfold increase in fifty years. But rapid industrialization failed to bring prosperity to the working class. Industrial laborers worked twelve-hour shifts six days a week. As late as 1910, Gary steel workers earned only seventeen cents an hour. Workers injured on the job received no compensation.

Looking for leadership, many working-class people turned to Eugene Debs, a union organizer from Terre Haute. Debs helped establish a gigantic labor union called the Industrial Workers of the World (IWW, or "Wobblies"). Under the banner of two different Socialist parties, Debs ran for president of the United

States in 1900, 1904, 1908, 1912, and 1920. A staunch opponent of American entry into World War I, Debs was thrown into jail as a traitor. While sitting in a prison cell in 1920, Debs received nearly one million votes in his bid for the presidency.

THE WINDS OF CHANGE

The demands of World War I increased factory output and pushed up crop prices. When peace came, however, crop prices dropped to below their prewar level, and hundreds of farm families faced bankruptcy. In the postwar years, farm families increasingly gave up their land to take factory jobs in Indianapolis, Muncie, Anderson, Fort Wayne, and South Bend. During the 1920s, the number of Hoosier city dwellers eclipsed that of rural people for the first time in the state's history.

In the World War I years and the early 1920s, a steady stream of blacks came from the South to Indiana. The number of blacks in the state rose from 60,000 in 1910 to 112,000 in 1930. The overwhelming majority of black newcomers sought factory jobs in Indianapolis and Gary. The blacks often found a bitter reception from white Hoosiers who had roots in the Old South. Of all the northern states, Indiana was said to have the "most southern" attitude toward race relations. Indiana maintained separate schools for blacks and whites until the 1940s. Southern Indiana cities required separate seating for the races at movie theaters. Blacks were forbidden to swim in the municipal pools of many communities.

In the 1920s, the white-hooded Ku Klux Klan made inroads in many states, northern and southern. In the Hoosier State, the Klan was headed by a powerful orator named D. C. Stephenson, who once declared, "I am the law in Indiana." Preaching against blacks

For a few years in the 1920s, the Indiana branch of the Ku Klux Klan (right), headed by D. C. Stephenson (above), was a powerful force in the state.

and the recently arrived European immigrants (most of whom were Catholic or Jewish), Stephenson and the Klan helped elect a number of public officials, including Governor Ed Jackson, in 1924. But the Klan had no lasting influence on Indiana government. Stephenson was convicted of a brutal murder and sentenced to prison. The *Indiana Times* waged an editorial war against the hooded group, and exposed the fact that Klan funds had been used to bribe state politicians. By the late 1920s, the Ku Klux Klan was a fading memory in the Hoosier State.

The Great Depression of the 1930s was a national disaster, but it brought especially hard times to Indiana. By 1932, one of every four Hoosier factory hands was out of work and collecting some sort of welfare. Farmers, who had never shared in the prosperity

The Great Depression of the 1930s brought poverty and unemployment to every part of Indiana.

of the 1920s, sank even deeper into debt. In southern Indiana, where workers were dependent on coal mining or limestone quarrying, unemployment climbed as high as 50 percent.

Hoosier voters turned to the Democratic party for depression relief. In 1932, Democrat Paul V. McNutt, the dean of Indiana University's Law School, won the governorship in a landslide vote. State government soon passed a series of laws giving compensation to the unemployed and relief money to the destitute. But while the 1930s was the decade of the Democrats, the most famous Hoosier politician was Republican businessman Wendell Willkie, who ran against Franklin Roosevelt in the 1940 presidential election. Willkie was defeated, but he polled more than 22 million votes.

During World War II, the Studebaker Corporation manufactured trucks, cars, and amphibious vehicles such as these for the war effort.

The onset of World War II pulled Indiana and the rest of the nation out of the grip of the depression. Early in the war, so many Studebaker trucks were sent from South Bend to Russia under the Lend Lease Act that the Russians grew to believe "Studebaker" was the American word for "truck." In southern Indiana, the war altered life in some towns forever. Evansville's population grew almost 50 percent during the war years, as workers flocked to the city's factories and shipyards. Gunpowder plants built at Charlestown helped increase the town's population fourfold. As is always the case, however, wartime prosperity came with a terrible price tag. More than ten thousand Hoosiers died in World War II.

INDIANA TODAY

Hoosier voters celebrated the end of World War II by sending arch-conservative William Jenner to the United States Senate, where he led a movement demanding the impeachment of President Harry S. Truman. In Washington, Jenner was joined by powerful Hoosier Republicans such as Senator Homer Capehart and Representative Charles Halleck. Backing those conservative politicans were the American Legion and the Indianapolis *Star*, owned by Eugene C. Pulliam.

Mirroring the rest of the nation, Indiana in the 1950s saw the spread of suburbs and the decline of traditional downtown shopping areas. Developers in Indianapolis began building the Glendale Shopping Center in 1953, and when completed, the mall lured thousands of shoppers away from the city's old downtown. Gary suffered from white flight as blacks moved in and whites fled to the suburbs. By 1960, Gary was almost 40 percent black.

Indiana made great strides in race relations during the decade of the 1950s. The first step toward civil rights was taken in 1949, when the legislature abolished the state's dual school system for blacks and whites. The normally conservative Indianapolis *Star* joined the civil-rights campaign. Indiana's victory over segregation was peaceful and it was lasting. During the violent 1960s, when at least one hundred American cities suffered race riots, no major disorders rocked Indiana.

The business community experienced progress as well as reversals during the 1960s. Fort Wayne thrived with factory expansion led by firms such as the International Harvester Company, General Electric, and Central Soya. The steel mills of Gary, on the other hand, grew old and could no longer compete successfully with foreign steelmakers. Tragedy reigned in South Bend as the Studebaker Company — the city's largest employer — suffered a disastrous sales slump. Studebaker was forced to shut down its auto-making plants in 1963, and thousands of South Bend workers lost their jobs. In other Hoosier cities, however,

In 1967, Richard G. Hatcher of Gary (right), shown here at a mayors' conference in Washington, D.C., became the first black mayor of a midsized American city.

auto making increased. General Motors, which owned nine plants in six Indiana cities, became the state's biggest single employer.

The voters of Gary chose Richard Hatcher to be their mayor in 1967. He was the first black to become mayor of a midsized American city. The new mayor inherited a city with a deteriorating downtown and high unemployment. Shortly after taking office, he said, "I am now the mayor of roughly ninety thousand black people, but we do not control the possibility of jobs for them, or money for their schools, or state-funded social services. Those things are in the hands of the United States Steel Corporation and the County Department of Welfare. Will the poor in Gary's worst slums be helped because the pawnshop owner is black, not white?"

Indianapolis expanded under a program called Unigov. Initiated by Republican Mayor Richard Lugar (who later became a United States senator), Unigov combined sixty local government agencies into six departments and enlarged the city limits to incorporate nearby suburbs. When Unigov took effect in 1970, the city added 300 square miles (777 square kilometers) to its area. In terms of

In the summer of 1987, some four thousand athletes from thirty-eight nations gathered in Indianapolis for the Pan American Games.

population, Indianapolis went from being the twenty-sixth largest city in the country to the eleventh largest overnight.

During the nationwide business recession of the early 1980s, the state's unemployment rate was one of the worst in the country. Unemployment approached 20 percent in Muncie and Anderson, ranking them among America's ten worst cities in terms of joblessness. The closing of International Harvester plants in Fort Wayne wiped out four thousand jobs. But the state's economy recovered in the second half of the 1980s as auto making and other traditional Hoosier industries revived. As one economist noted, "Indiana smokestack industries are by no means dead."

Throughout the 1980s, Indianapolis enjoyed a building boom, especially in sports and convention facilities. The sixty-thousand-seat Hoosier Dome and the smaller Market Square Arena were completed in the downtown region. The decade's most dramatic event was the Pan American Games, played in the summer of 1987. Some four thousand athletes from thirty-eight nations gathered in the Hoosier capital. Untold thousands of spectators came, too, and enjoyed traditional Hoosier hospitality.

Chapter 7

GOVERNMENT AND THE ECONOMY

GOVERNMENT AND THE ECONOMY

Indianapolis is, of course, the hub of government in the Hoosier State. But the city also has almost fifteen hundred factories that each year produce more than $2 billion in manufactured goods. In Indianapolis, as well as in the rest of the state, the government and private industry are partners in progress.

THE GOVERNMENT

Indiana is governed by its constitution, which was written in 1850 and has been amended many times since then. The constitution divides state government into three departments: executive, legislative, and judicial.

The executive branch is headed by the governor and is responsible for enforcing laws. The constitution gives the governor the power to appoint the heads of important state agencies. The governor and other major officers in the executive department—the lieutenant governor, the attorney general, the secretary of state, the auditor, and the treasurer—are elected to four-year terms.

The legislative branch is divided into two houses: a fifty-member senate and a one-hundred-member house of representatives. The legislature creates new laws and rescinds old ones. When both houses of the legislature approve a proposed law (called a bill) it is sent to the governor. If the governor signs the

Purdue University, in West Lafayette (above), and the University of Notre Dame, in South Bend (right), are two of Indiana's many institutions of higher learning.

bill it becomes a law. The governor may reject (veto) a bill, but the legislative department can override the governor's veto by repassing the bill with the majority vote of both houses. Most state constitutions require a two-thirds majority in order to override a governor's veto.

The judicial department is made up of the court system. State courts interpret laws and try cases. A five-member supreme court and a twelve-member court of appeals are the state's highest courts. New judges for both the supreme court and the court of appeals are appointed by the governor to serve two-year terms. After a two-year period, the new judge faces election, and if elected holds office for ten years. Indiana has ninety circuit courts and many county and local courts. The court system hears cases ranging from murders to petty thefts and from disputes between giant corporations to squabbles between neighbors.

Local government functions are administered by Indiana's 92 county, 115 city, and more than 1,000 township organizations. Local government controls vital services such as the funding of township police forces and the maintaining of parks and county roads.

Running the government of Indiana is a tremendously expensive operation. The state budget approaches $8 billion a year—a figure greater than the annual budget of many of the world's nations. How to raise and spend money is the subject of heated debate in government circles. State funds come primarily from a sales tax, an individual income tax, and a corporate income tax. The state also taxes such special items as gasoline, tobacco, and alcohol. The state lottery, begun in October 1989, is expected to become a major source of income.

EDUCATION

Providing for a school system is the costliest item in the state budget. Nearly one million students currently attend Indiana's public primary and secondary schools, at a cost of about $2,500 a year per student. According to state law, all children from the age of seven to sixteen must attend school.

In 1988, Indiana developed a unique program called A+ For Excellence in Education. Under the program, all students are tested in reading and math, and schools are graded on the basis of their students' test scores. In effect, each school is given its own "report card." United States Education Secretary William Bennett said the A+ program is "one of the best education reform [measures] that I have ever seen."

Hoosiers point with pride to their state's outstanding colleges and universities. Indiana University, with its main branch at Bloomington, is one of the nation's largest state-supported universities. Other major state-supported universities include Purdue, in West Lafayette; Ball State, in Muncie; and Indiana State, in Terre Haute. The state's largest private universities are Notre Dame, in South Bend; Butler, in Indianapolis; and the

Wheat being harvested in Tippecanoe County

University of Evansville. Well-known smaller private colleges
include DePauw, in Greencastle; Earlham, in Richmond; Hanover,
in Hanover; Valparaiso, in Valparaiso; Wabash, in
Crawfordsville; and the University of Indianapolis.

AGRICULTURE

Indiana consistently ranks among the nation's top ten states in
farm production. Income from farm products approaches
$5 billion a year. The state has about 88,000 farms, with an
average size of 192 acres (78 hectares).

Among the fifty states, Indiana ranks fifth in corn production,
fourth in the production of soybeans, and first in the production
of popcorn. Hoosiers also grow winter wheat, hay, tobacco, and
oats. Vegetable growers cultivate cabbage, cucumbers, and
potatoes. Major fruits harvested in the state include apples,
melons, and peaches.

Indiana is America's leading steel producer.

Indiana ranks thirteenth among the states in livestock and livestock products. More than 4 million hogs and 1.6 million cattle are raised in the state. About 200,000 dairy cows graze in the fields. Indiana is among the leading states in poultry and egg production.

MANUFACTURING

Manufacturing employs nearly 660,000 Hoosier men and women—the state's largest source of jobs. Among the fifty states, Indiana is America's leading steel producer. Giant steel mills, most of them in the Gary area, churn out 20 million short tons (18 million metric tons) of raw steel each year. One plant in Gary has the largest blast furnaces in the entire Western Hemisphere.

The manufacture of electrical equipment is the state's second-largest industry. Transportation equipment, which includes the production of cars, trucks, and vehicle parts, ranks third. Factories

A limestone quarry
in Delaware County

in Evansville, Fort Wayne, Bloomington, Anderson, and Kokomo
are major producers of electrical machines and transportation
equipment. Indianapolis is home to the Eli Lilly Company, a huge
manufacturer of prescription drugs. Other plants in the state
produce storage batteries, mobile homes, household furniture,
phonograph records and tapes, wooden office furniture, and
musical instruments.

MINING

Mining and quarrying give employment to more than 11,000
Hoosier men and women. In addition to quarrying limestone,
Indiana workers mine soft coal, sand, gravel, and natural gas.

Providing limestone blocks for buildings has become an
important industry in southern Indiana. After World War II,
many architects abandoned limestone blocks in favor of glass and
steel. But the use of limestone for large buildings became popular
again in the late 1980s.

TRANSPORTATION AND COMMUNICATION

True to its motto, "Crossroads of America," Indiana has more
miles of interstate highway than any other state of comparable

Indiana railroads carry millions of tons of freight each year.

size. Four major interstates pass through the Indianapolis region. All told, Indiana has more than 90,000 miles (144,837 kilometers) of roads.

About 6,600 miles (10,621 kilometers) of railroad track crisscross the Hoosier State. Railroads still carry millions of tons of freight, but passenger service is now limited to ten major cities. The state has 135 public airports and 326 private airports and heliports. The state's largest shipping port is Burns Harbor, in northwest Indiana. Completed in 1970, Burns Harbor unloads mountains of iron ore intended for the hungry blast furnaces of Gary. Indiana's second-most important port is the Southwind Maritime Center, located near Evansville on the busy Ohio River.

Indiana has about 70 daily newspapers, with a total circulation of more than 1 million copies. The state's largest newspaper is the Indianapolis *Star*. A number of magazines, including the *Saturday Evening Post* and *Children's Digest*, are published in Indiana. The state also has 250 radio stations and 35 television stations.

Chapter 8
ARTS AND ENTERTAINMENT

ARTS AND ENTERTAINMENT

Indiana writer George Ade once said, "Hoosier home folks are a good deal more sophisticated than they let on to be." His statement rings true when we examine Hoosier contributions to American art, sports, and especially literature.

THE FINE ARTS

The town of New Harmony was the educational and cultural capital of the Indiana frontier. Charles Alexander Lesueur taught painting and drawing at New Harmony, and he also made sketches of nearby settlers and settlements. The state's first artist of note was Englishman George Winter, who came to Indiana in 1837 and painted outstanding landscapes of the Wabash River country. During the Civil War years, Indianapolis resident Jacob Cox became a well-known artist and art teacher.

Near the turn of the century, the Brown County Artist Colony was formed in the town of Nashville. Members of the artists' group painted nature scenes inspired by the beautiful forested hills of southern Indiana. Theodore C. Steele was perhaps the most famous Brown County artist. Other art colonies developed in Richmond, Muncie, and South Bend. The style of artists such as William Forsyth, Otto Stark, and John Bundy came to be called the Indiana school of painting, which celebrated nature in romantic landscapes. This "Hoosier Group" made a profound impact on the art world of the era, and is enjoying a rebirth today. Influenced by the Indiana school were three black artists—Hale Woodruff, John Hardrick, and William Scott. Though the three worked in obscurity in the 1920s and 1930s, their paintings now hang in museums.

Modern Indiana boasts a lively art scene. According to the Indiana Arts Commission, 53 art associations and 108 craft shops operate within the state. One of the state's most influential modern artists is sculptor Robert Indiana, who was born Robert Clark but changed his name to demonstrate his Hoosier pride. Hoosiers Mary Beth Edelson and Robert Berkshire are two talented contemporary painters.

MUSIC AND THE PERFORMING ARTS

Indianan Paul Dresser wrote some of America's favorite songs. Dresser was the brother of writer Theodore Dreiser, who wrote the words to many of Paul's songs. Dresser's haunting song "On the Banks of the Wabash, Far Away" was adopted as the official state song in 1913.

The early 1900s saw the rise of ragtime and jazz—peculiarly American forms of music. Black musicians led the ragtime movement. One of ragtime's greats was Reginald DuValle, who played in clubs in Indianapolis's black district. DuValle's music influenced a young Indiana University student named Hoagy Carmichael. In the 1930s and 1940s, Carmichael wrote immensely popular songs, including "Star Dust" and "Georgia on My Mind." Another great Hoosier composer of the era was Cole Porter, who was born in Peru. Porter wrote the musicals *Kiss Me, Kate* and *Can-Can*, and the songs "Night and Day" and "Begin the Beguine."

Today, Indiana has music for everyone's taste. Thirty-one symphony orchestras and thirty-seven noncollege choral groups

Above: James Dean, born in Marion, was a popular
movie star of the 1950s.
Right: Indiana Repertory Theatre in Indianapolis

perform regularly in the state. The renowned Indianapolis
Symphony Orchestra is headquartered in Circle Theater, a
magnificently restored concert hall. Scores of young classical
musicians train at the Arthur Jordan College of Music, a part of
Butler University. Indianans are almost as passionate about their
high-school marching bands as they are about high-school
basketball teams. Marching-band contests draw crowds of fans.

Popular rock musician Michael Jackson grew up in a white
frame house on a street in the heart of Gary. The street is now
named Jackson after the famous musical family.

Theater also thrives in modern Indiana. Nashville is famed for
its open-air playhouse, where drama students from Indiana
University perform. Butler University hosts a popular summer
theater. An excellent professional group, the Indiana Repertory
Theatre, stages plays in a refurbished movie palace in downtown
Indianapolis.

Hoosiers have long starred in radio, television, and film. Phil
Harris, born in Linton, was a singer and radio host during the
1940s. James Dean, born in Marion, was a movie star of the 1950s.

Dean died in an auto crash at the age of twenty-four, but he became a cult figure for his roles as a brooding youth in such movies as *East of Eden* and *Rebel Without a Cause*. Comedian Red Skelton, born in Vincennes, starred in *A Southern Yankee, I Dood It, The Fuller Brush Man,* and other rollicking movies of the 1940s. Herb Shriner was a radio and television host who based many of his jokes on his love for Hoosierland. Shriner, who arrived in the state as a baby, said, "I was born in Ohio, but moved to Indiana as soon as I heard about it."

THE WORLD OF LITERATURE

Hoosier humorist and poet George Ade once told the story of a lecturer from the East who addressed an Indiana audience and noted that the state has produced a remarkable number of authors. The lecturer then announced, "If there are any authors present, I'd like them to come forward and sit on the stage with me." With a rumble of chairs, everyone in the audience, with the exception of one elderly man, stood and moved forward. The astonished lecturer pointed and said, "You mean every one of you but him is an author?" According to George Ade, a man standing near the lecturer replied, "Oh, he writes, too. But he's deaf and just didn't hear what you said."

What makes Hoosiers write? For decades, critics and literature professors have tried to answer that question. The experts have provided no satisfactory answers, but all agree that Indiana has spawned more great writers than any other comparably sized state.

The pioneer era's most celebrated writer was John Finley, who lived in Wayne County and published the poem "Hoosiers' Nest" in 1813. Finley was one of the first writers to popularize the nickname Hoosier. Edward Eggleston, who was born in the tiny village of Vevay, wrote poignantly about life on the Indiana frontier in his book *The Hoosier Schoolmaster*.

Poet James Whitcomb Riley was born in a two-room log cabin in Greenfield. In his youth, he was a sign painter and a laborer before he turned to poetry. Riley glorified his rural Indiana childhood in such poems as "The Old Swimmin' Hole," "Little Orphan Annie," and "When the Frost is on the Punkin'." One of Riley's most popular poems is this ode to his home state:

> Ain't God good to Indiana?
> Folks, a feller never knows
> Just how close he is to Eden
> Till sometimes, he ups and goes
> Seekin' fairer, greener pastures
> Than he has right here at home
> Where there's sunshine in the clover
> An' there's honey in the comb:
> Where th' ripples on th' river
> Kind o' chuckle as they flow;
> Ain't God good to Indiana?
> Ain't He, fellers? Ain't He, though?

The golden age of Indiana literature began in the late 1800s with the emergence of Riley, Frank Hubbard, George Ade, and Meredith Nicholson. Frank McKinney ("Kin") Hubbard wrote folksy "cracker-barrel" philosophy, and he sketched pictures for Indiana newspapers. Playwright and poet George Ade wrote humorous accounts of rural Indiana life. Meredith Nicholson's most famous work, *The Hoosiers*, is a study of Indiana history and society.

Two of the state's writers—Lew Wallace and Albert J. Beveridge—achieved fame in the literary world as well as in other fields. Lew Wallace, born in Brookville, was a Civil War general and the territorial governor of New Mexico; he also wrote the best-selling novel *Ben-Hur* about the rise of Christianity in the Roman Empire. Albert J. Beveridge was a United States senator from Indiana for twelve years. In 1920, Beveridge won the coveted Pulitzer Prize in biography for *The Life of John Marshall*, a biography of the Supreme Court justice.

Indiana's contributions to American literature continued in the early twentieth century with authors Booth Tarkington and Gene Stratton Porter. Booth Tarkington produced thirty-six novels and collections of short stories, including the Pulitzer Prizewinning *Magnificent Ambersons* and the popular *Gentleman from Indiana*. Gene Stratton Porter wrote best-selling sentimental novels such as *Freckles* and *The Girl of the Limberlost*.

One of America's great novelists of the early 1900s was Theodore Dreiser, who was born to a poor family in Terre Haute. Dreiser drew his characters from real life. For example, his most famous book, *An American Tragedy*, is based on an actual murder. Though his characters commit evil acts, Dreiser blames the acts on a wicked society rather than on the characters' weaknesses. His book *Sister Carrie* is the story of a young actress who grows rich, but cannot find happiness. *The Financier* tells of a businessman hungry for success.

Ernie Pyle, born in Dana, became the nation's most popular war correspondent during the World War II years. Pyle's newspaper columns and his books detailed the lives of ground-slogging foot soldiers facing the horrors of war. Also during the World War II period, Jean Shepard wrote his colorful story "County Fair," and Hoosier-born Mary Jane Ward exposed the barbarism of mental institutions in her novel *The Snake Pit*.

Modern Hoosier writers include Kurt Vonnegut, Jr., Ross Lockridge, Jr., Jessamyn West, and Irving Leibowitz. For years,

Two of Indiana's best-known writers are Jessamyn West, author of *The Friendly Persuasion*, and Kurt Vonnegut, whose novels include *Cat's Cradle* and *Slaughterhouse Five*.

Kurt Vonnegut was an obscure writer of science-fiction stories, but in the 1970s he captured public attention with novels such as *Cat's Cradle* and *Slaughterhouse Five*. Jessamyn West is best known for her moving novel *The Friendly Persuasion*, the story of an Indiana Quaker community. Ross Lockridge's historical novel *Raintree County* became a popular movie. Critic Irving Leibowitz wrote a bittersweet account of life in the Hoosier State in his book *My Indiana*.

SPORTS

Fans around the nation agree that the Indianapolis 500 is the greatest of all automobile races. The famed "Indy 500" is held every Memorial Day weekend and brings together the world's most daring drivers and the fastest machines. Crowds numbering as many as 300,000 throng into the Indianapolis Motor Speedway Stadium to watch the event. The race is two hundred laps, or 500 miles (805 kilometers), long. Spectacular crashes sometimes occur as drivers and machines roar around the course. The first Indy 500

The Indianapolis 500, held every year on Memorial Day weekend, draws crowds of as many as 300,000.

was held in 1911. In that initial race, the winner averaged about 75 miles (121 kilometers) per hour and collected a first-place "purse" worth $14,000. Today, the average speed surpasses 160 miles (257 kilometers) per hour, and the winner's purse is more than $3 million.

Aside from its famed speedway, Indianapolis is a center for many amateur sporting events. Track meets, bicycle races, wrestling matches, swimming meets, and endless other amateur sporting contests are held in the city. Swimming is a particularly competitive amateur sport in the Hoosier State. Indiana University's greatest swimmer was Mark Spitz, who splashed to seven gold medals in the 1972 Olympic Games. In the entire history of the Olympic Games, no other athlete has won so many gold medals in a single year.

Professional team sports in Indianapolis are represented by the Pacers of the National Basketball Association (NBA) and the Colts

The Indianapolis Colts play football in the Hoosier Dome.

of the National Football League (NFL). Both teams have produced exciting players. Explosive running back Eric Dickerson joined the Colts in 1987. Hoosier-born basketball great George McGinnis spent his last playing years with the Pacers.

College team sports in the Hoosier State have enjoyed dizzying success. For most of the twentieth century, Notre Dame has been a premier football power. Notre Dame fans have hailed star players such as Paul Hornung, Allan Page, Joe Montana, and Tim Brown. Legendary Notre Dame football coaches include Knute Rockne, Frank Leahy, and Ara Parseghian. Hoosier basketball fans have cheered—and winced—at Indiana University's coach Bobby Knight, who has fielded championship teams but has also thrown

Cross-country skiing (left) and long-distance foot racing (above) are among the sports enjoyed by Hoosiers.

outrageous temper tantrums on the basketball court. The most successful coach in college basketball history was John Wooden, who was born in Martinsville and became an all-American guard for Purdue. As head coach for UCLA, Wooden's teams won an unprecedented ten national championships during the 1960s and 1970s.

Hoosiers love sports at any and all levels, but high-school basketball occupies a special place in their passions. Fans talk in loving terms about stars of the past: Oscar Robertson of Indianapolis, Steve Alford of New Castle, or the amazing Larry Bird of French Lick. Fans muse over mighty teams such as East Chicago's Washington High, Indianapolis's Crispus Attucks High, and Muncie's Central High. But when lovers of Hoosier high-school basketball gather, the talk is bound to drift to the year 1954, when tiny Milan faced rugged Muncie Central for the state championship. The Milan five became high-school legends when Bobby Plump sank a last-second shot to capture the crown. The 1987 movie *Hoosier* dramatized this "Milan Miracle," and the game will forever stand as one of the greatest moments in the long and colorful history of Indiana sports.

Chapter 9

A TOUR OF INDIANA

A TOUR OF INDIANA

The Hoosier State has mighty industrial cities as well as quiet farming communities. Its towns are graced with parks, museums, and architectural surprises. It would take a lifetime to see all Indiana has to offer, but a brief tour might very well start in the north and work south.

NORTHWESTERN INDIANA

Northwestern Indiana is the state's most diverse region. It looks upon visitors with three faces: the industrialized cities of the Calumet, the lovely sand dunes on the Lake Michigan shore, and its many farms and villages.

Driving southeast out of Chicago, a traveler passes the cities of the Calumet—Whiting, East Chicago, Gary, and Hammond. The Calumet region is one of the world's greatest industrial centers, but the four cities do not present Indiana's prettiest face. Oil refineries, steel mills, cement plants, and countless factories spread from horizon to horizon with few trees or patches of greenery to break up the mechanical maze. The air hanging over the cities reeks with industrial pollution despite attempts in recent years to clean up emissions.

More than half a million people live in the Calumet region. While pollution and pockets of severe unemployment plague the cities, the people have built many tidy neighborhoods, and have

Gary's Genesis Convention Center, completed in 1981, hosts concerts, conventions, and sporting events.

fostered exciting institutions. Gary is the home of the Northwest Indiana Symphony Orchestra, and the city boasts the newly completed Genesis Convention Center. Visitors in Hammond journey one hundred years into the past as they tour the Joseph Hess Schoolhouse. Built in 1869, the schoolhouse contains its original bell.

Just east of the Calumet cities spread the lovely Indiana Sand Dunes. These restless mountains of sand with names such as Baldy, Jackson, and Tom, have served as a natural playground for generations of Hoosiers as well as neighboring Chicagoans. Visitors to the Indiana Dunes National Lakeshore and the Indiana Dunes State Park swim and explore in the summer and cross-country ski during the winter months. The park contains a 2,000-acre (809-hectare) reserve and offers guests a 3-mile- (5-kilometer-) long beach as well as dozens of hiking trails.

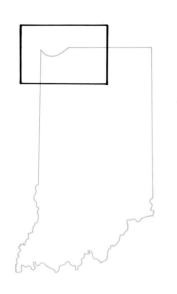

Children construct elaborate sand castles at the swimming beach in Michigan City's lakefront Washington Park.

Serving visitors to the sand dunes are the resort towns of Michigan City and La Porte. Pride of Michigan City is Washington Park, a 90-acre (36-hectare) lakefront gem with a swimming beach, picnic tables, and a zoo. La Porte boasts the Little Theater Company and the La Porte Symphony Orchestra.

Below the dunes area is Crown Point, famed for its century-old Court House Square. Near the square in Crown Point stands the old Lake County Jail from which, in 1934, Chicago gangster John Dillinger escaped by using a "pistol" he had carved from a wooden block. To the west is Valparaiso, seat of Porter County and home to Valparaiso University. At Valparaiso's William Cummings Museum of Electronics are radios dating back to the 1920s and aging jukeboxes that spin 78 rpm (revolutions per minute) records.

Two famous Indiana landmarks are Court House Square in Crown Point (left) and the golden dome that caps an early campus building at the University of Notre Dame (right).

South Bend is Indiana's fifth-largest city and a renowned cultural center. The Studebaker National Museum in South Bend houses classic Studebaker cars and the carriage Abraham Lincoln took to Ford's Theater the night he was assassinated. South Bend's Snite Museum of Art displays outstanding paintings, including a work by Pablo Picasso. The city's Discovery Hall documents South Bend's industrial history. No visit to South Bend is complete without a stroll on the University of Notre Dame campus. The campus spreads over 1,250 acres (506 hectares), embraces ninety buildings, and contains twin lakes and many wooded areas. Famous landmarks at Notre Dame are the great golden dome that caps the main campus building, and the Grotto of Our Lady of Lourdes, where students go to meditate or to pray.

NORTHEASTERN INDIANA

Northeastern Indiana is lake country, famed for its fishing. Fort Wayne is the northeast's leading industrial center. The region is also home to a large number of Amish, America's most successful farmers.

"Please touch," is the motto of the Mishawaka Children's Museum on the city's main street. Among the museum's "hands-on" exhibits are Indian artifacts and fossils that have been found in the area. In nearby Elkhart are the Midwest Museum of Art and an architectural wonder called the Ruthmere Mansion. To the south is the city of Nappanee, known for its woodworkers and its award-winning small-town library. Residents of Angola point with pride to their historic Public Square, where white settlers once traded goods with Potawatomi Indians. Far to the south is the city of Wabash, with its delightful collection of old houses and commercial buildings.

Dazzling lakes greet travelers in the northeast. Bluegill fishing is said to be superb at Lake Wawasee, near Warsaw. Huntington Lake, near Huntington; Salamonie Lake, near the town of Lagro; and Mississinewa Lake, near Peru, make up a lovely recreation area that invites hikers, fishing enthusiasts, and canoeists.

Kokomo is named after Miami chief Kokomo, whose monument still stands in the city. Kokomo was once the home of brilliant inventor Elwood Haynes, who developed America's first commercially successful automobile. The Elwood Haynes Museum in Kokomo is devoted to the work of this remarkable man. To the northwest is Peru, where Cole Porter was born and raised. Once known as the "Circus Capital of America," Peru draws visitors year-round to its fascinating Circus City Museum. Near the town of Bluffton spreads the 1,000-acre (405-hectare) Ouabache State

Visitors at historic Fort Wayne are entertained with tales of traders and voyageurs.

Park, one of nineteen state parks in Indiana, where hiking trails lead through lush marshlands. In Geneva stands the Limberlost Museum, an early home of Gene Stratton Porter, one of the state's favorite writers.

Fort Wayne, the state's second-largest city, is steeped in history. The city had its beginnings in 1794, when General "Mad Anthony" Wayne built a wilderness fort on the site. Visitors today tour a replica of the old fort's log barracks. The city's experience as a riverboat trading center is preserved at The Landing, a charming gaslit street on the old canal dock site. Fort Wayne's "Jazz Age" is frozen in its remarkable Embassy Theater, a jewel of a building constructed in 1928. Another of the city's interesting historical buildings is the Bass Mansion, now the St. Francis College Library.

Museums and cultural sites abound in Fort Wayne. The Fort Wayne Museum of Art displays its masterpieces in a magnificent Victorian manor house. Airplane buffs flock to the Greater Fort Wayne Aviation Museum. Abraham Lincoln artifacts are shown at the Louis A. Warren Lincoln Library and Museum. The Fort Wayne Zoo re-creates an African savanna with its 22-acre

(9-hectare) grasslands exhibit. Exotic plants bloom year-round at Fort Wayne's Foellinger-Freimann Botanical Conservatory, a huge expanse of greenery enclosed under glass. Flower lovers also tour the city's famous Lakeside Rose Garden. North of Fort Wayne, in Auburn, is the Auburn-Cord-Duesenberg Museum, a delight for lovers of antique cars.

Taking the rural roads in northeastern Indiana, a traveler will no doubt see a horse and buggy driven by a black-clad Amish farmer. Without the help of tractors or other power tools, Amish farmers have prospered by working the raw land as did their ancestors centuries ago. At markets in towns such as Middlebury, Shipshewana, and Nappanee, Amish families sell delicious maple syrup, molasses, and apple butter made the old-fashioned way. The gentle clip-clopping of Amish buggies over roads so close to industrial Fort Wayne reminds visitors that the Hoosier State is a place of fantastic variety.

CENTRAL INDIANA

Indiana's great central belt contains the state's best farmland and many lively midsized towns. Graceful architecture, historic sites, and scenic landscapes all merge in the central region of Hoosierland.

In Fountain City stands the Levi Coffin House, once a vital link on the Underground Railroad. One of the two thousand or more escaped slaves who rested at the Coffin House was Eliza, the heroine of Harriet Beecher Stowe's novel *Uncle Tom's Cabin*. Visitors at the Whitewater Canal are thrust into the past when they board a boat and ride over the canal as did the pioneers more than a hundred years ago. In nearby Connersville, tourists climb aboard another time-honored vehicle—an old steam-driven train.

Conner Prairie is a re-creation of an 1836 pioneer village.

On the streets near downtown Muncie are row after row of gorgeous century-old houses. Some of the houses have lapsed into a sorry state of repair, but many have been neatly restored. The Ball Corporation left Muncie an important legacy. Rare glass jars are displayed at the Ball Corporation Museum, and precious works of art hang at the Ball State University Art Gallery. The nearby city of Dunkirk also has a glass museum where early pieces are displayed.

Art galleries and a small theater add spice to Anderson's historic West 8th Street, a national preservation area with restored nineteenth-century homes and gaslights. Also in Anderson is the Victorian Gruenwald Home, built in 1870. A short drive from downtown Anderson is Mounds State Park, with eleven mounds and earthworks. Northwest of Anderson is the city of Atlanta, which residents claim is an antique lover's paradise.

The boyhood home of James Whitcomb Riley, Indiana's favorite poet, is in Greenfield. One of central Indiana's most popular tourist spots is Conner Prairie Pioneer Settlement, in Noblesville. The settlement is a thirty-building living-history museum that takes guests back to a pioneer village typical of the early 1800s.

99

Covered bridges greet the traveler in Parke and Montgomery counties. Most of the bridges are closed to automobile traffic, but they stand as handsome relics of the Midwest's past. Crawfordsville, in Montgomery County, was the home of Henry S. Lane, a powerful politician in Civil War times. Lane's restored house is a highlight of the town.

To the north are Lafayette and West Lafayette, home of Purdue University. At the town of Battle Ground, just north of Lafayette, a monument commemorates the victory of William Henry Harrison over warriors led by Tecumseh's brother, the Prophet. The Greater Lafayette Museum of Art holds more than three hundred paintings and pieces of sculpture. Lafayette also has the Columbia Park Zoo and the enchanting Clegg Memorial Gardens, which border Wildcat Creek.

Shades State Park, near Alamo, and Turkey Run State Park, near Rockville, are two of central Indiana's wilderness playgrounds. Shades attracts canoe enthusiasts who paddle along the scenic Sugar Creek and camp in an area reserved for canoeists. Hiking through beautiful sandstone canyons is the major appeal of Turkey Run State Park. Turkey Run offers ten hiking trails that range from easy to rugged.

INDIANAPOLIS

Millions of cross-country travelers pass through the Indianapolis area each year, but many fail to stop and see the capital city. Travelers who take the time to explore Indiana's largest city find many delightful surprises.

In the very center of Indianapolis stands the Soldiers and Sailors Monument. Rising 250 feet (76 meters) above its base, the carved limestone shrine was completed in 1901. At its top stands a heroic

Highlights of central Indiana include the many covered bridges in Parke County, such as this one in Turkey Run State Park (top right); the elaborate Soldiers and Sailors Monument in Indianapolis (above); and the neoclassical Tippecanoe County Courthouse in Lafayette (right).

sculpture of Lady Victory, who looks south toward the old Confederacy in a gesture of reconciliation. The nearby Indiana War Memorial honors the state's war veterans. Also in the heart of downtown is the splendid state capitol, built of Indiana limestone. Inside is a grand hall, three stories in height, which extends the length of the building. The massive building was completed in 1888, after builders worked on it for ten years.

Indianapolis (left) is proud of the refurbished interior of Union Station (above), the historic railroad depot that now contains more than a hundred restaurants and shops.

Indianapolis has an exciting array of museums. The Indiana State Museum invites guests to take a walk through history—past woolly mammoths, a scene of the Indiana wilderness as it appeared three hundred years ago, and an 1890s Indianapolis street scene. The Children's Museum of Indianapolis has a saying, "Here children grow up and adults don't have to!" The Children's Museum invites kids to try on clothes from different eras and from faraway lands, and to look for buried clues at an archaeological dig. Row after row of shiny antique racing cars greets visitors at the Indianapolis Motor Speedway Museum.

The fine arts enjoy a devoted following in the Hoosier capital. The Herron Gallery is a center for contemporary art. The Indianapolis Museum of Art has a superb oriental collection. The Eiteljorg Museum, which opened in 1989, specializes in American Indian and western art. Young artists exchange ideas and show their works at the Indianapolis Art League. The Center for the Creative Arts Gallery is a cooperative venture run by artists.

More than 130 parks add to Indianapolis's charm. Sprawling White River State Park is the city's major downtown playground. In the park is the 64-acre (26-hectare) grounds of the Indianapolis Zoo, where some two thousand animals live in settings that simulate their natural habitat.

Among the many historic structures in Indianapolis is the Benjamin Harrison Home, where prized possessions of the twenty-third president are displayed in the ballroom. The neighborhood called Woodruff Place is a collection of vintage houses connected by tree-lined boulevards. The liveliest of the town's older buildings is Union Station, a historic railroad depot that has been converted to a festive marketplace containing more than a hundred restaurants and shops.

SOUTHERN INDIANA

Dramatic changes greet the traveler in southern Indiana. The flat cornfields of the north give way to rugged bluffs, deep forests, and even an occasional waterfall. The south is also a region rooted in history.

Terre Haute's Early Wheels Museum displays old vehicles ranging from racing cars to bicycles. The Terre Haute home of labor leader Eugene Debs has been turned into a museum that traces the history of working men and women. North of Terre Haute is Dana, where the home of war correspondent Ernie Pyle attracts many visitors.

Southeast of Terre Haute is Bloomington, headquarters of Indiana University. Bloomington's Lilly Library holds thousands of rare books, including a copy of the Gutenberg Bible. Limestone quarrying is big business in towns such as Ellettsville and Needmore, near Bloomington. Outside Needmore is water-filled

Many visitors to the Nashville area make a charming inn their headquarters while they participate in the many activities Brown County has to offer.

Empire Hole, where the limestone that went into New York's Empire State Building was quarried. The delightful 1979 movie *Breaking Away*, which told of the rivalry between quarry-working families (called cutters) and middle-class college students, was filmed in the Bloomington area.

For nearly a hundred years, Nashville and the splendid forests of Brown County have inspired the state's artists. On fall days, when nature works its magic on the trees, people still set up easels and paint. Arts and crafts shows are frequent events throughout Brown County. For people who love to shop, Nashville's more than 250 shops provide a marvelous array of merchandise.

To the south, near Bedford, is Bluespring Caverns, where boats take guests on an underground tour of Myst'ry River. Tour boat passengers gasp at the caverns' subterranean splendors.

Covering almost 200,000 acres (80,938 hectares), the sprawling Hoosier National Forest is the state's largest tract of public land. The rugged forest, which extends north from the Ohio River, offers hiking, horseback riding, boating, and many other outdoor activities. On the southern end of the forest, near the town of Curby, is the Wyandotte Cave. One of many fascinating limestone caves in the region, Wyandotte contains what is perhaps the largest underground mountain in the United States.

Spring Mill State Park, near the town of Mitchell, features a reconstructed pioneer village complete with a water-powered gristmill. A little south is the town of French Lick, home of the Indiana Railroad Museum. Train buffs enjoy climbing aboard the museum's six locomotives and more than twenty-one antique railroad cars.

Versailles State Park, near Versailles, is a 5,900-acre (2,388-hectare) wilderness adventureland. The bicycle paths that cut through the heart of Versailles State Park draw cyclists from miles around. Near Vernon is the Brush Creek State Fish and Wildlife Area, which is made up of ten small lakes ringed by forests.

Madison is the queen of Ohio River cities. Rambling old houses line block after block in this historic river town. According to a city pamphlet, "Nowhere in the middle west is it possible to find architecture that rivals Madison." Famous structures include the Sullivan House, built in 1818; an awesome Greek Revival mansion called the Shrewsbury House; and the J. F. D. Lanier Mansion, which is now a state historic site.

The colorful history of the Ohio River region can be studied at New Albany's Floyd County Museum. History also comes to life at Corydon, Indiana's first state capital. In Corydon stand the restored capitol building and the home of William Hendricks, Indiana's third governor.

Certainly we all know that Abraham Lincoln rose to fame as a resident of Illinois, but Indiana claims the great man, too. Lincoln lived in southern Indiana from 1816 to 1830. The sixteenth president is honored at the Lincoln Pioneer Village, near Rockport, and he is remembered in the play *Young Abe Lincoln,* performed at Lincoln City.

The people of Evansville, a city situated on a horseshoe bend of the Ohio, have long had a special love for the river. Strollers in Riverside and Sunset parks watch powerful barges and delicate pleasure boats churn through the water. Evansville's Museum of Arts and Sciences exhibits items as diverse as a stagecoach once driven by Calamity Jane and a peace pipe owned by Sitting Bull. Also in Evansville is the ancient earthwork complex called Angel Mounds. Central Mound, part of the complex, is one of the largest prehistoric structures in North America.

New Harmony, on the Wabash River, lives with its soul in the past but its heart and mind in the culture of tomorrow. Tour guides in the town take visitors through the twenty-four-building site constructed more than 150 years ago by idealists trying to carve a Utopia in the wilderness. But it is a mistake to think of New Harmony as a relic of the past. It remains an active cultural center, with modern paintings hanging at the New Harmony Gallery of Contemporary Art. Residents and guests also enjoy concerts at the city's Music Center and plays at the New Harmony Theater. As was true in the past, New Harmony remains the state's most interesting small town.

Vincennes, also on the Wabash River, is Indiana's oldest town. Some historians believe that the French built a trading post at Vincennes as early as 1683. The town was the capital of the old Northwest Territory, and the two-room frame building that served as the territorial government's only office still stands. Also preserved in Vincennes is Grouseland, the home of William Henry Harrison, the territorial governor and the ninth president of the United States. Near downtown Vincennes rises the lovely

The centerpiece of the George Rogers Clark National Memorial is a statue of the man who was instrumental in obtaining the Northwest Territory for the United States.

George Rogers Clark National Memorial. Clark, the conqueror of Fort Sackville, has been a Hoosier hero for more than two hundred years.

Vincennes ends a tour of Indiana. The Hoosier State contains stunning architecture, historical sights, cultural centers, and nature preserves. Most important, it is a society of people proud of their communities and proud of their state. In this land of poets, Hoosier Sarah T. Bolton expressed the sentiments of her people well in these lines:

> The winds of heaven never fanned
> The circling sunlight never spanned
> The borders of a better land
> Than our own Indiana.

FACTS AT A GLANCE

GENERAL INFORMATION

Statehood: December 11, 1816, nineteenth state

Origin of Name: Named for the people who lived there, Indiana means "Land of the Indians"

State Capital: Indianapolis, capital since 1825

State Nickname: Hoosier State

State Flag: The Indiana flag has nineteen gold stars and a gold torch on a blue field. The torch represents liberty and enlightenment. The rays represent the far-reaching influence of liberty and enlightenment. The stars in the outer circle represent the thirteen original states. Those in the inner circle represent the next five states admitted to the Union. The largest star, above the torch, stands for Indiana, the nineteenth state. Indiana's flag was adopted in 1917.

State Motto: Crossroads of America

State Bird: Cardinal

State Flower: Peony

State Tree: Tulip tree

State Stone: Indiana limestone

State Seal: The seal depicts a pioneer woodsman felling a tree while a buffalo runs from the forest; the sun is setting behind the hills in the background.

State Song: "On the Banks of the Wabash, Far Away," words and music by Paul Dresser, adopted as the state song in 1913.

> Round my Indiana homestead wave the cornfields,
> In the distance loom the woodlands, clear and cool.
> Oftentimes my thoughts revert to scenes of childhood,
> Where I first received my lessons, nature's school.
>
> Oh, the moonlight's fair tonight along the Wabash,
> From the fields there comes the breath of new-mown hay.
> Through the sycamores the candlelights are gleaming
> On the banks of the Wabash, far away.

POPULATION

Population: 5,490,260, twelfth among the states (1980 census)

Population Density: 151 people per sq. mi. (58 people per km²)

Population Distribution: 65 percent of Indiana's people live in cities or towns. More than 50 percent of the people live in or near the capital city of Indianapolis.

Indianapolis	700,807
Fort Wayne	172,349
Gary	151,953
Evansville	130,496
South Bend	109,727
Hammond	93,714
Muncie	77,216
Anderson	64,695
Terre Haute	61,125
Bloomington	52,044

(Population figures according to 1980 census)

Population Growth: Indiana has shown steady and sometimes spectacular growth over the years. The state's population nearly doubled between 1840 and 1860, nearly doubled again between 1860 and 1900, and more than doubled between 1900 and 1970. Like other midwestern states, Indiana experienced less growth in population than the national average from 1970 to 1980. The state's population increased 5.7 percent over that decade, while the United States as a whole gained 11.4 percent.

Year	Population
1820	147,178
1840	685,866
1860	1,350,428
1880	1,978,301
1900	2,516,462
1920	2,930,390
1940	3,427,796
1950	3,934,224
1960	4,662,498
1970	5,195,392
1980	5,490,260

GEOGRAPHY

Borders: States that border Indiana are Ohio on the east, Kentucky on the south, Illinois on the west, and Michigan on the north. Lake Michigan borders Indiana for 40 mi. (64 km) on the northwest.

An evening view of the Ohio River between Indiana and Kentucky

Highest Point: Franklin Township, in Wayne County — 1,257 ft. (383 m)

Lowest Point: Ohio River, in Posey County — 320 ft. (98 m)

Greatest Distances: North to south — 275 mi. (443 km)
East to west — 160 mi. (257 km)

Area: 36,291 sq. mi. (93,994 km²)

Rank in Area Among the States: Thirty-eighth

Rivers: The majestic, slow-moving Wabash River, which flows through the center of the state and forms the southwestern border, is Indiana's longest river. The Wabash and its main tributaries, the White and Tippecanoe rivers, drain two-thirds of the state. The Wabash flows into the Ohio River, which forms Indiana's southern boundary. Most of the state's rivers flow southward and westward into the Ohio, and eventually, into the Mississippi. In the northeast, the St. Joseph joins the St. Marys River at Fort Wayne to form the Maumee River, which flows into Lake Erie. Two other northern rivers, the Pigeon and Elkhart, flow into Lake Michigan.

Lakes: Most of Indiana's natural lakes are found in the northern third of the state. They formed from melting prehistoric glaciers. Lake Wawasee, at 5 sq. mi. (13 km²), is the largest of such lakes in Indiana. Other natural lakes include Manitau, Maxinkuckee, and Turkey. Monroe Lake, in the southern part of the state, is the largest man-made lake, covering 29 sq. mi. (75 km²).

The Portland Arch Nature Preserve, near Fountain

Shoreline: Indiana has 40 mi. (64 km) of shoreline along Lake Michigan. Of that, 15 mi. (24 km) is taken up by industries and another 15 by the Indiana Dunes National Lakeshore and the Indiana Dunes State Park. The rest is business or residential property.

Topography: Indiana has three main land divisions. The Great Lakes Plains forms a lowland that borders the Great Lakes shoreline. This region covers the northern quarter of the state. Many small lakes formed by glaciers are found here. Sand dunes border Lake Michigan. South of the dunes lies farmland of fertile black soil.

The central plains, or Till Plains, cover the heart of the state. This fertile agricultural region contains till, or rows of debris, left by glaciers. Most of the Till Plains is level, but some low hills and shallow valleys exist.

The Southern Hills and Lowlands region comprises the most scenic portion of the state. Geologists and nature lovers appreciate this land of hills, sharp ridges, rounded knobs, valleys, steep bluffs, natural bridges, caves, and waterfalls.

Climate: Indiana, like most of the Midwest, experiences hot summers and cold winters. The growing season varies from 150 days in the north to 200 days in the south. Average January temperatures vary from 25° F. (-4° C) in South Bend to 35° F. (2° C) in Evansville. Average July temperatures range from 73° F. (23° C) in South Bend to 78° F. (26° C) in Evansville. Long dry periods as well as floods occasionally occur in the southern parts of the state, and tornadoes are a potential spring and summer danger.

Wildflowers that grow in Indiana include goldenrod (above), violets (top right), and buttercups (right).

NATURE

Trees: Black gums, southern cypresses, white pines, jack pines, maples, oaks, ashes, beeches, maples, sycamores, hickories, elms, butternuts, mulberries, catalpas, yellow poplars (tulip trees)

Wild Plants: Persimmons, floating pondweeds, pitcher plants, peppermints, tulips, strawberries, raspberries, huckleberries, blackberries, violets, buttercups, anemones, sweet williams, daisies, goldenrod, sunflowers

Animals: Red foxes, beavers, otters, muskrats, raccoons, squirrels, deer, opossums

Birds: Teals, mallards, blue herons, thrushes, larks, warblers, sparrows, robins, woodpeckers, blue jays, bluebirds, cardinals, wrens, quail, whippoorwills, wild turkeys, mourning doves

Fish: Catfish, pickerel, bass, sunfish, bluegills, crappies

GOVERNMENT

Indiana has had two constitutions in its history. The first was adopted at statehood in 1816. The second was framed by members of a constitutional convention and was approved by the voters in 1851.

Like the federal government, Indiana's government is divided into three branches: legislative, executive, and judicial. The legislative branch (General Assembly) consists of a 50-member senate and a 100-member house of representatives. The state has 50 senate districts, each of which elects one senator, and 77 representative districts, each of which elects from one to three representatives. Senators serve four-year terms. Representatives serve two-year terms.

The executive branch consists of the governor and lieutenant governor (who are elected as a team), attorney general, secretary of state, auditor, and treasurer. All serve four-year terms. The governor, secretary of state, auditor, and treasurer may not serve more than two terms in a row. The governor has the power to appoint and dismiss the heads of nearly all state institutions and to establish the salaries of those officials based on the state budget.

The judicial branch is made up of the court system. The supreme court consists of a chief justice and four associate justices. A nonpartisan judicial commission chooses the chief justice from among the five supreme court justices. The court of appeals has twelve judges. New supreme court and appeals court judges are appointed by the governor for two-year terms. Voters then decide whether to retain them for ten-year terms. Circuit court judges serve six-year terms. Some counties also have superior and special courts. Judges on these courts serve four-year terms.

Number of Counties: 92

U.S. Representatives: 10

Electoral Votes: 12

Voting Qualifications: United States citizen, at least eighteen years of age, must be registered to vote thirty days before an election

EDUCATION

Education has always been an important goal in Indiana. The state's first constitution established a general system of education from the township level up to and including a state university "wherein tuition be gratis [free] and equally open to all." Despite this far-reaching aim, most schools in the state's early history were private or church-owned. Many educational experiments were tried in the early days, and some are in use today. The New Harmony community was the first in the country to teach boys and girls together. The colony also had one of the first nursery schools.

At first, Indiana had many small school districts. A reorganization act in 1959 consolidated many of these smaller districts. A 1949 law forbade segregation in public education.

A state board of education directs the school system. The eleven-member body consists of the superintendent of public instruction and ten other members. Voters elect the superintendent of public instruction to a four-year term. The governor appoints the other board members to four-year terms.

There are about 1 million public school students. Another 100,000 attend private schools. It costs the taxpayers about $2,500 a year to educate each public school student. Students must attend school from age seven to sixteen.

Indiana has about forty universities and colleges, which are attended by about 250,000 students. Indiana University, considered one of the finest state universities in the country, is the largest. Its main campus is in Bloomington, with others in Gary (IU Northwest), Kokomo, New Albany (IU Southeast), Richmond (IU East), and South Bend. Indiana University-Purdue University has campuses in Fort Wayne and Indianapolis. Purdue University has its main campus in West Lafayette and others in Hammond (Calumet Campus) and Westville (North Central Campus). Ball State University, in Muncie; Indiana State University, in Terre Haute; and the University of Southern Indiana, in Evansville, are other large state universities.

Other colleges and universities include Anderson College, in Anderson (Church of God); Bethel College, in Mishawaka (Missionary Church); Butler University, in Indianapolis; Calumet College, in Whiting (Roman Catholic); DePauw University, in Greencastle; Earlham College, in Richmond (Quaker); University of Evansville, in Evansville; Fort Wayne Bible College, in Fort Wayne; Franklin College of Indiana, in Franklin; Goshen College, in Goshen (Mennonite); Grace Theological Seminary, in Winona Lake (Brethren); Hanover College, in Hanover; Huntington College, in Huntington (United Brethren in Christ); Indiana Institute of Technology, in Fort Wayne; Manchester College, in North Manchester (Brethren); Marian College, in Indianapolis (Roman Catholic); Marion College, in Marion (Wesleyan); University of Notre Dame, in South Bend (Roman Catholic); Oakland City College, in Oakland City; Rose-Hulman Institute of Technology, in Terre Haute; St. Francis College, in Fort Wayne (Roman Catholic); St. Joseph's College, in Rensselaer (Roman Catholic); St. Mary-of-the-Woods College, in St. Mary-of-the-Woods (Roman Catholic); St. Mary's College, in South Bend (Roman Catholic); St. Meinrad College and St. Meinrad School of Theology, in St. Meinrad (Roman Catholic); Taylor University, in Upland; Tri-State University, in Angola; University of Indianapolis, in Indianapolis; Valparaiso University, in Valparaiso (Lutheran); and Wabash College, in Crawfordsville.

ECONOMY AND INDUSTRY

Principal Products:

Agriculture: Soybeans, poultry, vegetables, corn, beef cattle, dairy cattle, potatoes, grapes, dairy products, hay, hogs, oats, fruit, sheep, tobacco, barley, wheat, eggs, turkeys

Manufacturing: Electric machinery and equipment, phonographs, transmission equipment, television and radio equipment, steel, transportation equipment,

Gary's steel industry is concentrated at the shore of Lake Michigan.

chemicals, nonelectric machinery, food products, farm machinery, oil refining, rubber and glass products, surgical implants, musical instruments, baseball bats
  Natural Resources: Limestone, natural gas, coal, clay, sand and gravel, gypsum, forest products, oil

Business: Most of Indiana's gross state product (GSP)—59 percent—comes from service industries. Wholesale and retail trade are the most valuable service industries. They account for 16 percent of the GSP. Finance, insurance, and real estate account for another 13 percent. Much of this revenue comes from the sixty-five life insurance companies that have their headquarters in Indiana. Community, social, and personal services account for 12 percent of the GSP, and government accounts for 9 percent. Transportation, communication, and utilities make up another 9 percent.

Industry accounts for 41 percent of the GSP. Much of this total comes from manufacturing (34 percent). The industry total also includes construction (4 percent) and mining (2 percent). Agriculture makes up 1 percent of the GSP.

Indianapolis, a meat-packing center, also serves as headquarters of such "white-collar" industries as insurance. The American Legion and the world-famous *Saturday Evening Post* magazine have their headquarters here. The Calumet area, in the northwest region of the state, is one of the most important steel-producing regions in the country. Evansville and Fort Wayne are also important trading centers. Much of the state's trade is conducted through the large neighboring cities of Chicago, Cincinnati, and Louisville.

I-90, shown here near Hammond, is one of Indiana's major highways.

Communication: Indiana's first newspaper, the *Indiana Gazette*, was published in Vincennes in 1804. Its first dailies, the *Journal* (now the Indianapolis *Star*) and the *Sentinel*, appeared in Indianapolis in 1851. Indiana now has about 250 newspapers, including about 70 dailies. About 190 periodicals are published in the state. The Indianapolis *Star* is the largest newspaper. Other important papers include the *Indianapolis News*, the *South Bend Tribune*, and the *Fort Wayne Journal Gazette*.

WSBT, owned by the *South Bend Tribune*, took to the airwaves in 1921 as the first commercial Indiana radio station. WTTV-TV, in Bloomington, and WFBM-TV (now WRTV-TV), in Indianapolis, were the first Indiana television stations, in 1949. Indiana now has about 250 radio stations and 35 television stations.

Transportation: Since statehood, Indiana has had a sound basis for claiming the name "Crossroads of America." Then and now, Indiana has been a transportation hub. In the early years, river traffic, especially along the Ohio, was the major means of transport. That changed as rail and road traffic became more important. The National Road (later U.S. Highway 40) was a major westward migration route.

Today, Indiana is a major interstate highway hub. I-80 and I-90 cross the northern portion of the state. Four major interstate highways—65, 69, 70, and 74—meet in Indianapolis. Interstate 64 crosses the southern portion of the state.

About 25 railroads serve Indiana on about 6,600 mi. (10,621 km) of track. Passenger trains serve about ten Indiana cities. Indiana has about 135 public airports, and hundreds of small, private airports. Ports on Lake Michigan ship goods throughout the world. Burns Harbor in Portage is the largest such port. Others include Gary and East Chicago. Smaller ports on the Ohio River enable the shipping of goods along the Mississippi River system.

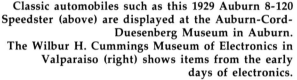

Classic automobiles such as this 1929 Auburn 8-120 Speedster (above) are displayed at the Auburn-Cord-Duesenberg Museum in Auburn. The Wilbur H. Cummings Museum of Electronics in Valparaiso (right) shows items from the early days of electronics.

SOCIAL AND CULTURAL LIFE

Museums: The varied aspects of Indiana life are well captured in the state's many museums. The Indiana State Museum in Indianapolis contains exhibits of Indiana art, state history, natural history, and Indian lore. The capital city also claims one of the finest children's museums in the country, which has Egyptian mummies, a dinosaur exhibit, toy trains, a performing-arts theater, and a replica of a limestone cave. The Indianapolis Museum of Art is a leading regional art museum. The Evansville Museum of Arts and Sciences contains a planetarium, a steam train, and a reconstructed turn-of-the-century village, plus art, history, and science exhibits. Indiana University and the University of Notre Dame have noted art museums. Fort Wayne and South Bend also have impressive art museums.

Other Indiana museums contain interesting and specialized collections. The Speedway Museum honors the famous Indianapolis 500 auto race. The House of Clocks Museum in French Lick displays timepieces dating from the early 1800s. The Wilbur H. Cummings Museum of Electronics in Valparaiso shows items from the early days of electronics, such as old telegraph systems, spark transmitters, and jukeboxes. The Louis A. Warren Lincoln Library and Museum, in Fort Wayne, is a storehouse of Abraham Lincoln material. Peru houses a circus museum. The Auburn-Cord-Duesenberg Museum at Auburn is a treasure trove of antique cars.

Libraries: Indiana's first public subscription library opened in Vincennes in 1807. By the 1850s, the state had more than 600 small libraries. Now there are about 240 public libraries. The largest state library, containing about 3.9 million volumes, is at Indiana University at Bloomington. The Indiana State Library, at Indianapolis, houses the state archives and also has an extensive genealogical collection. The Indianapolis Public Library has a large collection of books by Indiana authors. Indiana University's Lilly Library is renowned for its rare books. The Old Cathedral Library, in Vincennes, contains books dating back to the 1800s.

Performing Arts: The Indianapolis Symphony Orchestra is the leading orchestra in the state. Indiana University's opera workshop attracts many visitors. Nashville's Brown County Playhouse attracts summer stock performers from Indiana University. Colleges and universities throughout the state host musical, dramatic, and dance events throughout their school years.

Sports and Recreation: Perhaps you think of "Cheer, cheer for old Notre Dame" and golden-helmeted Fighting Irish football players when you think of Indiana sports. Or maybe you recall the basketball mania that sweeps the state every winter. Many people believe Indiana has the best high-school basketball in the country. Indiana University is a frequent NCAA basketball champion, with Notre Dame not far behind in talent. In the 1960s, Indiana University's swimming team led the nation, and in the 1980s, the school dominated in soccer. Each Memorial Day weekend, Indianapolis hosts the Indy 500, the most famous auto race in the nation. The South Bend White Sox are a popular minor-league baseball team. Indianapolis also has two major-league sports teams: football's Indianapolis Colts and basketball's Indiana Pacers.

Nature lovers can roam in many areas of the Hoosier State. The huge Hoosier National Forest, with 188,000 acres (76,082 hectares), is located near Bedford. There are also dozens of state parks, state forests, and state fish and wildlife areas. Indiana visitors may hunt for quail, squirrels, deer, raccoons, and rabbits, or fish in one of the more than 1,000 lakes. Boating, canoeing, and swimming are other popular water sports. More adventurous souls may want to explore some of the many caves in the southern part of the state.

Historic Sites and Landmarks:

Corydon Capitol State Historic Site, in Corydon, is the blue limestone building that served as the state capitol from 1816 to 1825.

Council Oak Tree, in South Bend, is a 400-year-old tree under which French explorer La Salle met with Miami and Illinois Indians.

Fort Ouiatenon, in West Lafayette on the Wabash River, is a reconstruction of a 1719 French trading post; the museum on the site holds a wealth of information on the French, English, American, and Indian struggles for control of the Wabash Valley.

George Rogers Clark National Historic Park, in Vincennes, honors the famous Revolutionary War general; its centerpiece is a memorial building that contains murals of the highlights of Clark's career.

Historic Fort Wayne, in Fort Wayne, is a reconstruction of the log barracks of the 1815-19 period, with artifacts of General "Mad Anthony" Wayne and Chief Little Turtle; costumed guides furnish information on the soldiers and settlers of the period.

James Whitcomb Riley Birthplace, in Greenfield, was the boyhood home of the beloved Hoosier poet.

Levi Coffin House, in Fountain City, is the brick home of a husband and wife who helped more than two thousand fugitive slaves get to Canada and freedom via the Underground Railroad.

Lincoln Boyhood National Memorial, in Lincoln City, contains the original cabin in which Abraham Lincoln lived from the age of seven to twenty-one; also on the grounds is the grave of Lincoln's mother, Nancy Hanks Lincoln, and a living-history farm of the period.

New Harmony, on the Wabash River, is a restored and revitalized nineteenth-century experimental community in which members tried to establish a new social order to benefit mankind.

President Benjamin Harrison Memorial Home, in Indianapolis, was the residence of the twenty-third president.

Tippecanoe Battlefield and Museum, at Battle Ground, is the site of the 1811 battle in which a force led by General William Henry Harrison defeated Indians led by the brother of famed Shawnee leader Tecumseh.

Whitewater Canal State Historic Site, at Metamora, includes a restored section of the Whitewater Canal, which was heavily traveled in the early 1800s, and historic *Old Metamora,* a restored canal town with a working gristmill; visitors may tour a 14-mi. (23-km) stretch of the canal aboard a horse-drawn canal boat.

Other Interesting Places to Visit:

Amish Acres, in Nappanee, is an 80-acre (32-hectare) restored Amish living-history farm where maple syrup, apple cider, sorghum molasses, and dried foods are still produced and where Amish crafts such as quilting, rug weaving, and candle dipping are demonstrated; also on the grounds are an excellent Amish restaurant, food and craft shops, and a theater that produces *Plain & Fancy,* a musical depicting Amish customs.

Indianapolis Union Station is a national historic landmark.

Cathedral of the Immaculate Conception, in Fort Wayne, is known for its fine Gothic wood carvings.

East Race Waterway, in South Bend, is the only man-made white-water raceway in North America.

Indiana Dunes National Lakeshore, between Gary and Michigan City, contains sandy beaches, huge sand dunes, bogs and marshes, and hundreds of species of plants and animals; among activities visitors enjoy are swimming, fishing, boating, dune climbing, hiking, and horseback riding.

Indiana War Memorial, in Indianapolis, is a five-block plaza containing buildings, statues, flags, and fountains honoring Indiana soldiers through the years.

Indianapolis Motor Speedway, in Indianapolis, is the home of the world-famous Indianapolis 500 automobile race.

Indianapolis Union Station, in Indianapolis, is a national historic landmark that has been renovated to a marketplace containing more than a hundred shops and restaurants.

Madonna of the Trails, near Richmond, is a statue that honors pioneer women.

Mesker Park Zoo, in Evansville, has more than four hundred species of animals plus a reproduction of Columbus's flagship, the *Santa Maria*.

Mounds State Park, near Anderson, contains the remains of eleven earth formations built by early woodland Indians more than two thousand years ago.

Nashville, a scenic small town in Brown County, contains an active artists' colony and many shops that sell artworks and handicrafts.

Old Bag Factory, in Goshen, is a restored nineteenth-century factory that now houses artists' studios, an eighteenth-century blacksmith shop, a furniture-making studio, and shops that sell beautiful handcrafted items.

Parke County, in the west-central part of the state, contains thirty-four covered bridges, more than any other county in the country; the tourist information center in a restored train station in Rockville will supply a map for a tour of the bridges that span Raccoon and Sugar creeks.

State House, in Indianapolis, is a Corinthian structure of Indiana limestone with a copper dome that has served as the Indiana capitol since 1888.

Whitewater Valley Railroad, near Connersville, offers a scenic excursion on a steam train through the Whitewater Valley from Connersville to the historic canal town of Metamora.

Wyandotte Caves, near Leavenworth, is one of the largest cavern complexes in the United States, with five levels covering 35 mi. (56 km) of underground passageways.

IMPORTANT DATES

About 8000 B.C. — The first human beings arrive in the Great Lakes region

1679 — René-Robert Cavelier, Sieur de La Salle, travels along the St. Joseph and Kankakee rivers seeking a route to the Pacific Ocean

1717 — Fort Ouiatenon, an early French fortification, is completed

1732 — Vincennes, the first permanent Indiana settlement, is founded

1763 — The French cede the Northwest Territory and other regions to the British after the French and Indian War

1774 — The Quebec Act incorporates the Indiana area into the Province of Quebec

1779 — George Rogers Clark captures Vincennes from the British

1783 — Britain cedes land east of the Mississippi River to the United States

122

This two-story frame building in Vincennes was the capitol of Indiana Territory from 1800 to 1813.

1787 — Indiana becomes part of the Northwest Territory under the Northwest Ordinance

1794 — In the Battle of Fallen Timbers, General Anthony Wayne defeats the Miamis and other tribes; Wayne builds Fort Wayne to protect Indiana settlers from hostile Indians

1800 — Congress creates the Indiana Territory, with Vincennes as the capital

1804 — The *Indiana Gazette*, the first Indiana newspaper, begins publication

1805 — The Shakers establish a short-lived commune a few miles north of Vincennes

1809 — William Henry Harrison buys about 2,900,000 acres (about 1,170,000 hectares) of Indiana Territory land from the Indians for the United States

1811 — Harrison defeats the Shawnee confederation at the Battle of Tippecanoe

1813 — Corydon becomes the territorial capital; Indian leader Tecumseh dies in the Battle of Thames

1816 — Indiana enters the Union as the nineteenth state

1818 — The federal government buys lands in the central part of the state from the Indians and gives those lands to the state of Indiana

1820 — The site of present-day Indianapolis is chosen for the new state capital; Indiana Seminary, later Indiana University, is chartered

1825 — Indianapolis becomes the state capital; Robert Owen establishes a Utopian colony at New Harmony

1837 — DePauw University, originally called Asbury College (one of the state's oldest private colleges), opens

1838 — The last Potawatomis are driven from Indiana

1841 — William Henry Harrison is sworn in as the ninth president of the United States; he dies after only thirty days in office

1842 — The University of Notre Dame is founded

1852 — The Studebaker brothers begin building wagons

1861 — Abraham Lincoln, who spent his boyhood in Indiana, becomes the sixteenth president of the United States

1862 — Richard Gatling, of Indianapolis, invents a rapid-fire machine gun

1863 — Confederate troops led by General John Hunt Morgan raid southern Indiana

1869 — Schuyler Colfax takes office as vice-president of the United States under President Ulysses S. Grant

1881 — A provision barring blacks from the state is removed from the Indiana constitution; the American Federation of Labor (AFL) organizes in Terre Haute

1885 — Thomas Hendricks takes office as vice-president of the United States under President Grover Cleveland; he dies shortly afterward

1886 — Natural gas is discovered near Portland; the Ball brothers found a glass products company in Muncie

1888 — The present state capitol building is completed

1889 — Benjamin Harrison becomes the twenty-third president of the United States; the Standard Oil Company builds Indiana's first oil refinery plant, at Whiting

1894 — Elwood G. Haynes designs one of the first successful gasoline-powered cars

1905 — Charles Fairbanks takes office as vice-president of the United States under President Theodore Roosevelt

1911 — The first Indianapolis 500 race is held

1913 — Thomas Marshall begins serving the first of two terms as vice-president of the United States under President Woodrow Wilson

1915—Indiana adopts the Workmen's Compensation Act and the direct primary election law

1920—Albert Beveridge wins the Pulitzer Prize in biography for *The Life of John Marshall*

1921—WSBT, the state's first commercial radio station, begins broadcasting

1929—Robert Lynn publishes *Middletown, A Study in Contemporary Culture*, using Muncie as a model

1933—The state government reorganizes to give the governor greater powers over state agencies

1934—Harold Urey, of Walkerton, wins the Nobel Prize in chemistry for his discovery of the hydrogen isotope known as deuterium

1937—Ohio River flooding causes many deaths and extensive property damage

1944—Ernie Pyle wins the Pulitzer Prize in foreign correspondence for his war reporting

1949—The Indiana legislature passes a law requiring the desegregation of public schools

1956—The Northern Indiana Toll Road opens

1959—The General Assembly reorganizes the state school system, consolidating small school districts

1963—Indiana adopts a 2 percent sales tax

1965—The state creates the Department of Natural Resources to preserve land

1966—Indiana Dunes National Lakeshore is established

1967—Richard Hatcher becomes the mayor of Gary, one of the first black mayors of a major American city

1968—Frank Borman and two other astronauts become the first human beings to orbit the moon

1970—Indianapolis merges with Marion County under the Unigov program; the Port of Indiana in Burns Harbor opens, linking the harbor to the St. Lawrence Seaway; Paul Samuelson wins the Nobel Prize in economics

1976—Indiana University wins the first of three NCAA basketball championships under coach Bobby Knight

1982—Katie Hall, the first black United States representative from Indiana, enters Congress

1985—President Ronald Reagan appoints former Indiana governor Otis Bowen secretary of Health and Human Services

1989—Hoosier native Dan Quayle takes office as vice-president of the United States under President George Bush; the Indiana State Lottery is introduced

IMPORTANT PEOPLE

GEORGE ADE

BIRCH BAYH, JR.

George Ade (1866-1944), born in Kentland; humorist; described and poked fun at country people who moved to the city; wrote books of satirical fables and plays; created the comic opera *The Sultan of Sulu,* which enjoyed success on Broadway

Gordon Willard Allport (1897-1967), born in Montezuma; psychologist; studied personality appraisal and social psychology; theorized that a person's actions were determined by individual motives instead of heredity

Johnny Appleseed (1774-1847), born John Chapman; planter; walked through Ohio, Indiana, and Illinois territories, planting apple seeds as he walked; became a frontier and American folk legend

Arthur M. Banta (1877-1946), born in Greenwood; zoologist; gained scientific renown for his studies of environmental effects on cave animals

Birch Evans Bayh, Jr. (1928-   ), born in Terre Haute; lawyer, politician; U.S. senator (1963-81); won nationwide attention for his opposition to the Vietnam War; played a key role in the adoption of the Twenty-fifth and Twenty-sixth Amendments to the U.S. Constitution

Charles Austin Beard (1874-1948), born in Knightstown, and **Mary Ritter Beard** (1876-1958), born in Indianapolis; historians; wrote *The Rise of American Civilization* and other important studies of American history; he is considered the leading American historian of his era

Albert Jeremiah Beveridge (1862-1927), politician, historian; U.S. senator from Indiana (1899-1911); a leader of the Progressive Republicans; drafted a meat-inspection bill, fought for child-labor legislation, and voted against high tariff rates; won the 1920 Pulitzer Prize in biography for *The Life of John Marshall*

John Shaw Billings (1838-1913), born in Switzerland County; physician, librarian; expanded the Surgeon General's Library from 600 items to more than 50,000

Larry Joe Bird (1956-   ), born in French Lick; professional basketball player; is considered one of the game's all-time greats; many-time all-star for the Boston Celtics and led the team to three National Basketball Association (NBA) championships

LARRY BIRD

Frank Borman (1928-   ), born in Gary; astronaut, airline executive; commanded the first spaceflight to orbit the moon (1968); chairman of the board, Eastern Airlines (1976-   )

Otis Ray "Doc" Bowen (1918-   ), born near Rochester; physician, public official; became the first Indiana governor to serve two consecutive terms (1973-81); U.S. secretary of Health and Human Services (1985-89)

Mordecai Peter Centennial "Three Finger" Brown (1876-1948), born in Nyesville; professional baseball player; starred as pitcher with Chicago Cubs despite loss of two fingers in an accident; won 20 or more games six consecutive years; led Cubs to four pennants and two world championships; elected to the Baseball Hall of Fame

FRANK BORMAN

Ambrose Everett Burnside (1824-1881), born in Liberty; army officer, inventor, politician; invented breech-loading rifle; commanded troops in the Army of the Potomac during the Civil War; his beard style became origin of the term "sideburns"; governor of Rhode Island (1866-69); U.S. senator (1875-81)

AMBROSE BURNSIDE

Hoagland Howard (Hoagy) Carmichael (1899-1981), born in Bloomington; songwriter; composed hundreds of songs, including the classics "Stardust" and "Georgia on My Mind"; won a 1951 Academy Award for "In the Cool, Cool, Cool of the Evening"

William Merritt Chase (1849-1916), born in Nineveh; painter; founded the Chase School (later named the New York School of Art); painted landscapes and well-to-do Americans at the turn of the century

HOAGY CARMICHAEL

SCHUYLER COLFAX

EUGENE DEBS

VIRGIL GRISSOM

WILLIAM HENRY HARRISON

Schuyler Colfax (1823-1885), politician; U.S. representative from Indiana (1855-69); speaker of the house (1863-69); vice-president of the U.S. (1869-73)

James Robert (Jim) Davis (1945-   ), born in Marion; cartoonist; creator of the Garfield comic strip

James Byron Dean (1931-1955), born in Marion; actor; became famous for portrayals of intense, rebellious young men; starred in *Giant, East of Eden,* and *Rebel Without a Cause*

Eugene Victor Debs (1855-1926), born in Terre Haute; labor leader; formed the American Railway Union; was one of the founders of the Industrial Workers of the World (IWW, or "Wobblies"); led the 1894 Pullman strike; condemned World War I in his speeches; ran five times for the U.S. presidency as a Socialist

George Frederick Dick (1881-1967), born in Fort Wayne; physician; isolated the bacterium that causes scarlet fever

Theodore Dreiser (1871-1945), born in Terre Haute; writer; described characters who are victims of pressures from an uncaring society; wrote *An American Tragedy* and *Sister Carrie*

William Hayden English (1822-1896), born in Lexington; politician; U.S. representative (1853-61)

Weeb Ewbank (1907-   ), born in Richmond; football coach; won NFL championships with Baltimore Colts and New York Jets; coached the Jets to the 1969 Super Bowl championship

Charles Warren Fairbanks (1852-1918), born in Indianapolis; politician; U.S. senator (1897-1905); U.S. vice-president (1905-09)

Robert Allen (Bob) Griese (1945-   ), born in Evansville; professional football player; quarterback who led Purdue to the 1967 Rose Bowl championship; elected to the College Football Hall of Fame (1966); quarterback for the Miami Dolphins team that won the 1973 and 1974 Super Bowls

Virgil Ivan "Gus" Grissom (1926-1967), born in Mitchell; astronaut; flew on the second American spaceflight (1961); made the first two-man spaceflight, with John Young (1965); died in a spacecraft during preparations for the first three-man flight

Benjamin Harrison (1833-1901), twenty-third president of the United States (1889-93); U.S. senator from Indiana (1881-87); as president, he enacted civil-service reform, strong protective tariffs, the regulation of railroads, and the Sherman Antitrust Act; he signed legislation admitting Wyoming, North Dakota, South Dakota, Montana, Idaho, and Washington into the Union

William Henry Harrison (1773-1841), ninth president of the United States (1840); governor, Territory of Indiana (1800-12); defeated Indians at Battle of Tippecanoe (1811); U.S. representative from Ohio (1816-19); U.S. senator from Ohio (1825-28); died after only thirty days as president

Richard Hatcher (1933-), born in Michigan City; politician; mayor of Gary (1967-87), one of the first black mayors of a big city

John Milton Hay (1838-1905), born in Salem; diplomat, author; U.S. secretary of state (1898-1905); established the Open Door Policy, which allowed all western nations to trade in China

Thomas Andrews Hendricks (1819-1885), politician; U.S. representative from Indiana (1851-55); U.S. senator (1863-69); governor (1872); U.S. vice-president (1885)

Gilbert (Gil) Hodges (1924-1972), born in Princeton; professional baseball player, manager; first baseman for the Brooklyn and Los Angeles Dodgers; played on seven pennant-winning teams; managed "miracle" New York Mets to the 1969 World Series championship

James Riddle (Jimmy) Hoffa (1913-1975?), born in Brazil, Indiana; labor leader; president of Teamsters Union (1958-71); imprisoned for misusing union pension funds (1967-71); disappeared in 1975, believed murdered

Frank McKinney "Kin" Hubbard (1868-1930), born in Brown County; caricaturist, humorist; on staff of Indianapolis *News* (1891-94, 1901-30); created the rustic philosopher character Abe Martin

Michael Jackson (1958-), born in Gary; singer, dancer, songwriter; started his career with his brothers in the Jackson Five; his album "Thriller" was the biggest-selling album ever recorded

Jonathan Jennings (1784-1834), first governor of Indiana (1816-22); led the movement to transfer the capital from Corydon to the newly created city of Indianapolis

Thomas Edward (Tommy) John, Jr. (1943-), born in Terre Haute; professional baseball player; pitched for the Cleveland Indians, Chicago White Sox, Los Angeles Dodgers, New York Yankees, California Angels, and Oakland A's; won more than 280 major-league games, including three 20-game seasons

David Letterman (1944-), born in Indianapolis; graduate of Ball State University; television host known for his offbeat comedy

Little Turtle (1752-1812), born near Eel River; Miami Indian chief; led Miami Indians in battles against United States troops; signed a treaty in 1795 that opened southern Ohio to white settlement

Richard Green Lugar (1932-), born in Indianapolis; politician; mayor of Indianapolis (1968-75); U.S. senator (1977-); exerted pressure on Philippine dictator Ferdinand Marcos to hold free elections in that country

Thomas Riley Marshall (1854-1925), born in North Manchester; politician; governor (1909-13); U.S. vice-president (1913-21)

RICHARD HATCHER

JIMMY HOFFA

MICHAEL JACKSON

RICHARD LUGAR

STEVE McQUEEN

ROBERT OWEN

JANE PAULEY

DAN QUAYLE

Steve McQueen (1930-1980), born Terence Stephen McQueen in Indianapolis; actor; starred in such films as *The Great Escape* and *The Magnificent Seven*

Oliver Hazard Perry Throck Morton (1823-1877), born in Salisbury; politician; governor (1861-67); U.S. senator (1867-77); raised money to support Indiana troops when legislature refused to fund them

James Oliver (1823-1908), inventor, industrialist; designed and manufactured the first chilled-steel plow; president of the Oliver Chilled Plow Works of South Bend

Robert Owen (1771-1858), social reformer; founded a society in New Harmony that emphasized cooperation over competition; promoted education for children and better working conditions for women

Robert Dale Owen (1801-1877), social reformer; worked with his father in the New Harmony community; U.S. representative from Indiana (1843-47); Minister to Naples (1855-58); led the fight for the emancipation of black slaves

Jane Pauley (1950-   ), born in Indianapolis; television journalist; hosted television's "The Today Show"

Cole Porter (1891-1964), born in Peru; songwriter; gained fame for his romantic lyrics; wrote classic songs "Begin the Beguine," "Night and Day," and "I've Got You Under My Skin" and musicals such as *Kiss Me, Kate* and *High Society*

Ernest Taylor (Ernie) Pyle (1900-1945), born near Dana; journalist; wrote stirring accounts of World War II fighting; won 1944 Pulitzer Prize in correspondence for his reporting; killed in action during the Okinawa campaign

James Danforth (Dan) Quayle (1947-   ), born in Indianapolis; politician; U.S. representative from Indiana (1977-81); U.S. senator (1981-89); U.S. vice-president (1989-   )

James Whitcomb Riley (1849-1916), born in Greenfield; poet; known as the "Hoosier Poet"; wrote poetry in dialect that extolled the joys of Indiana; among his collections were *The Old Swimmin' Hole, 'Leven more Poems, Rhymes of Childhood,* and *Poems Here at Home*

Oscar Robertson (1938-   ), professional basketball player; starred at Crispus Attucks High School, in Indianapolis; played on the 1960 Olympic team; set scoring and assist records at the University of Cincinnati and with the NBA Cincinnati Royals and Milwaukee Bucks

Solon Robinson (1803-1880), social leader; organized Squatters' Union to protect squatters against land speculators and became known as "King of the Squatters"; founded Crown Point

Knute Kenneth Rockne (1888-1931), football coach; head coach of the University of Notre Dame football team from 1918 until his death in an airplane crash; delivered inspirational halftime speeches; under his coaching, the "Fighting Irish" won 105 games, lost only 12, and tied 5 for the highest winning percentage (.881) in history

Edd Roush (1893-   ), born in Oakland City; professional baseball player; a hard-hitting and slick-fielding outfielder for the Cincinnati Reds; won two National League batting championships; led Cincinnati to a World Series victory in 1919; elected to the Baseball Hall of Fame (1962)

Paul Anthony Samuelson (1915-   ), born in Gary; economist; won the 1970 Nobel Prize in economics; wrote *Foundations of Economic Analysis*, which showed the underlying unity of many economic theories

Red Skelton (1913-   ), born Richard Skelton in Vincennes; comedian; starred in radio, movies, and television; created imaginative characters such as Clem Kadiddlehopper, Freddie the Freeloader, Cauliflower McPugg, Bolivar Shagnasty, and Willie Lump Lump

David Roland Smith (1906-1965), born in Decatur; sculptor; created massive iron and metal forms that influenced later generations of artists

Rex Todhunter Stout (1886-1975), born in Noblesville; writer; created the colorful detective Nero Wolfe; wrote *Too Many Crooks, Some Buried Caesar*, and *A Family Affair*

Clement Studebaker (1831-1901) and **John Studebaker** (1833-1917), wagon and carriage manufacturers; started transportation business by making wagons in South Bend; the company later built Studebaker automobiles and trucks

Newton Booth Tarkington (1869-1946), born in Indianapolis; novelist, dramatist; among his books are *The Gentleman from Indiana* (1899); *Penrod* (1914); *Seventeen* (1917); *The Magnificent Ambersons*, which won the 1919 Pulitzer Prize in fiction; and *Alice Adams*, which won the 1922 Pulitzer Prize in fiction; his works described the wholesome life of the Midwest

Twyla Tharp (1941-   ), born in Portland; dancer and choreographer; composer of dances that feature movements from ballet, social dances, and tap dancing; her pieces are accompanied by music that ranges from ballet to rock and roll

Harold Clayton Urey (1893-1981), born in Walkerton; chemist; conducted work on isotopes and on the chemical nature of the solar system; won the 1934 Nobel Prize in chemistry for his discovery of deuterium, a hydrogen isotope

KNUTE ROCKNE

PAUL SAMUELSON

REX STOUT

TWYLA THARP

WENDELL WILLKIE

Willis Van Devanter (1859-1941), born in Marion; jurist; associate justice of the U.S. Supreme Court (1911-37); known for his conservative opinions

Kurt Vonnegut, Jr. (1922-   ), born in Indianapolis; writer; among his books are *Slaughterhouse Five, Cat's Cradle,* and *Breakfast of Champions*

Lewis (Lew) Wallace (1827-1905), born in Brookville; soldier and author; fought in the Mexican War; rose to the rank of major general in Civil War; blocked Confederate troops from capturing Washington, D.C.; wrote *Ben-Hur*

Jessamyn West (1907-1984), born in Indiana; writer; her novels, stories, screenplays, and essays emphasize the ideals of brotherhood; wrote *The Friendly Persuasion,* a story that described Quaker life in the mid-1800s

Wendell Lewis Willkie (1892-1944), born in Elwood; lawyer, politician, financier; financial wizard who became known as the "Barefoot boy of Wall Street"; opposed Franklin Roosevelt and the New Deal; won the 1940 Republican nomination for president but lost the election to Roosevelt

GOVERNORS

Jonathan Jennings	1816-1822	James A. Mount	1897-1901
Ratliff Boon	1822	Winfield T. Durbin	1901-1905
William Hendricks	1822-1825	J. Frank Hanly	1905-1909
James B. Ray	1825-1831	Thomas R. Marshall	1909-1913
Noah Noble	1831-1837	Samuel M. Ralston	1913-1917
David Wallace	1837-1840	James P. Goodrich	1917-1921
Samuel Bigger	1840-1843	Warren T. McCray	1921-1924
James Whitcomb	1843-1848	Emmett Forest Branch	1924-1925
Paris C. Dunning	1848-1849	Ed Jackson	1925-1929
Joseph A. Wright	1849-1857	Harry G. Leslie	1929-1933
Ashbel P. Willard	1857-1860	Paul V. McNutt	1933-1937
Abraham A. Hammond	1860-1861	M. Clifford Townsend	1937-1941
Henry Smith Lane	1861	Henry F. Schricker	1941-1945
Oliver P. Morton	1861-1867	Ralph F. Gates	1945-1949
Conrad Baker	1867-1873	Henry F. Schricker	1949-1953
Thomas A. Hendricks	1873-1877	George N. Craig	1953-1957
James D. Williams	1877-1880	Harold W. Handley	1957-1961
Isaac P. Gray	1880-1881	Matthew E. Welsh	1961-1965
Albert G. Porter	1881-1885	Roger D. Branigin	1965-1969
Isaac P. Gray	1885-1889	Edgar D. Whitcomb	1969-1973
Alvin P. Hovey	1889-1891	Otis R. Bowen	1973-1981
Ira Joy Chase	1891-1893	Robert D. Orr	1981-1989
Claude Matthews	1893-1897	Evan Bayh	1989-

Topography

MAP KEY

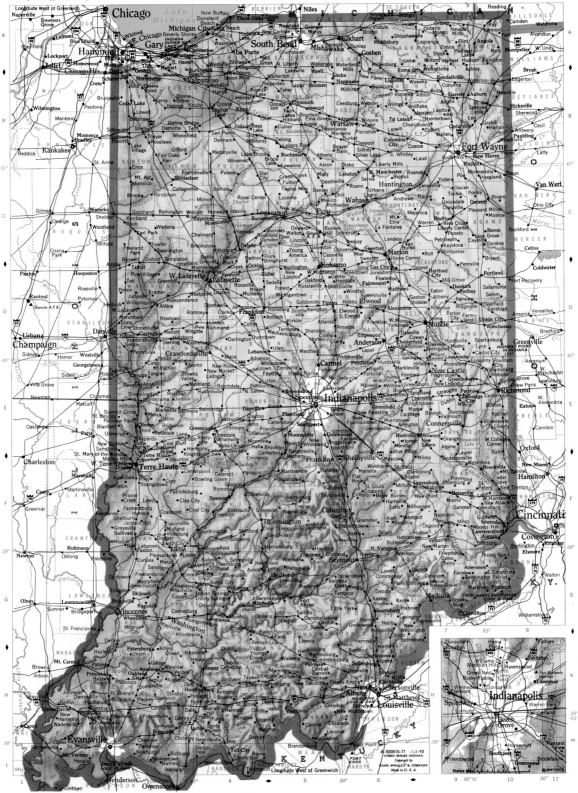

Lambert Conformal Conic Projection

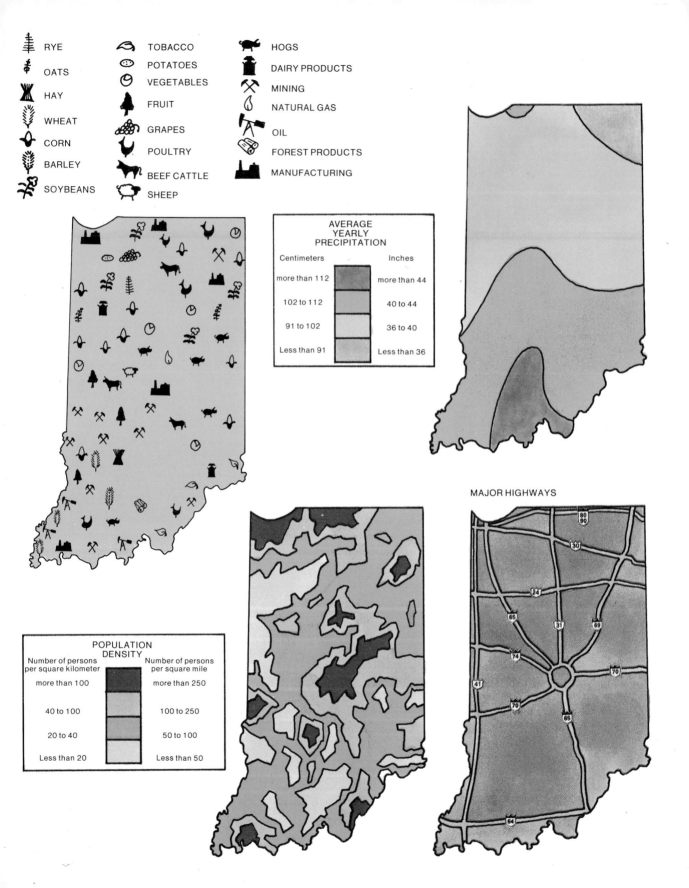

RYE

OATS

HAY

WHEAT

CORN

BARLEY

SOYBEANS

TOBACCO

POTATOES

VEGETABLES

FRUIT

GRAPES

POULTRY

BEEF CATTLE

SHEEP

HOGS

DAIRY PRODUCTS

MINING

NATURAL GAS

OIL

FOREST PRODUCTS

MANUFACTURING

AVERAGE YEARLY PRECIPITATION

Centimeters		Inches
more than 112		more than 44
102 to 112		40 to 44
91 to 102		36 to 40
Less than 91		Less than 36

MAJOR HIGHWAYS

POPULATION DENSITY

Number of persons per square kilometer		Number of persons per square mile
more than 100		more than 250
40 to 100		100 to 250
20 to 40		50 to 100
Less than 20		Less than 50

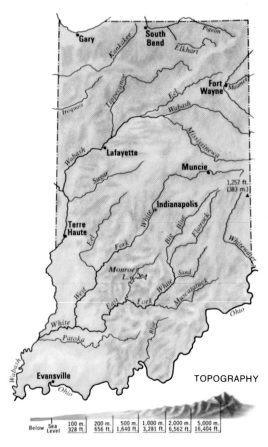

TOPOGRAPHY

| Below Sea Level | 100 m. 328 ft. | 200 m. 656 ft. | 500 m. 1,640 ft. | 1,000 m. 3,281 ft. | 2,000 m. 6,562 ft. | 5,000 m. 16,404 ft. |

Courtesy of Hammond, Incorporated
Maplewood, New Jersey

COUNTIES

A northern Indiana farm

INDEX

Page numbers that appear in boldface type indicate illustrations

Dune Creek, Indiana Dunes State Park

Picture Identifications

Front cover: The Huffman Bridge, built in 1880, which spans Big Walnut Creek in Putnam County
Back cover: Indiana Dunes State Park
Pages 2-3: Sand Lake, in Chain O'Lakes State Park
Page 6: Michigan City lighthouse
Pages 8-9: A country road in Rockville, Parke County
Page 18: Montage of Indiana residents
Page 24: *The Fall of Fort Sackville*, an oil painting by Frederic C. Yohn depicting the British surrender of Fort Sackville to George Rogers Clark
Pages 38-39: An early depiction of New Albany
Pages 52-53: An oxygen furnace in operation at J & L Steel Company, East Chicago
Page 70: The Indiana State House
Pages 78-79: *Oaks at Vernon*, an 1887 oil painting by Theodore Clement Steele, one of the Indiana Group artists
Pages 90-91: A night view of Indianapolis, with fireworks
Page 108: Montage showing the state flag, the state tree (tulip tree), the state flower (peony), and the state bird (cardinal)

About the Author

R. Conrad Stein was born in Chicago and graduated from the University of Illinois. He is the author of many books, articles, and short stories written for young readers. Mr. Stein lives in Chicago with his wife and their daughter, Janna. While growing up, Mr. Stein often visited the Hoosier State. To prepare for this book, he spent many enjoyable days traveling about Indiana. He wishes especially to thank the staff of the Indiana State Museum in Indianapolis for their courtesy.

Picture Acknowledgments

Front cover, © Ken Dequaine Photography/**Third Coast Stock Source;** 2-3, © Cathlyn Melloan/**TSW-Click/Chicago Ltd.;** 4, © **James P. Rowan;** 5, © Lee Balterman/**Marilyn Gartman Agency;** 6, © J. Madeley/**Root Resources;** 8-9, © Cathlyn Melloan/**TSW-Click/Chicago Ltd.;** 11, © Peter Pearson/**TSW-Click/Chicago Ltd.;** 12, © **Cathlyn Melloan;** 14 (left), © Robert Falls/**Photo Options;** 14 (right), © **James P. Rowan;** 15 (left), © **Lynn M. Stone;** 15 (right), © **Reinhard Brucker;** 16 (left), © **Cathlyn Melloan;** 16 (right), © **Reinhard Brucker;** 18 (top left), © James P. Rowan/**TSW-Click/Chicago Ltd.;** 18 (bottom left), © David Haynes/**Photo Options;** 18 (top right), © **Cathlyn Melloan;** 18 (middle right), © **Jeff Greenberg;** 18 (bottom right), © Cathlyn Melloan/**TSW-Click/Chicago Ltd;** 21, © Cathlyn Melloan/**TSW-Click/Chicago Ltd.;** 22, © MacDonald Photog./**Root Resources;** 24, **Courtesy of Indiana Historical Bureau, State of Indiana;** 27 (left), © **Clark Ray;** 27 (right), **Glen Black Laboratory of Archaeology, Indiana University, Bloomington;** 28, **M. & M. Karolik Collection, Courtesy of Museum of Fine Arts, Boston;** 30 (left), © **Cathlyn Melloan;** 30 (right), **Tippecanoe County Historical Society;** 33, © **George Rogers Clark Memorial;** 34 (left), **Smithsonian Institution;** 34 (right), **Historical Pictures Service, Chicago;** 35, © Cathlyn Melloan/**TSW-Click/Chicago Ltd.;** 36, **Historical Pictures Service, Chicago;** 37 (both pictures), © **James P. Rowan;** 38-39, **North Wind Picture Archives;** 41, © Georgia McGuire/**Journalism Services;** 42, **Joslyn Art Museum, Omaha, Nebraska;** 43, © **Jeff Greenberg;** 44, © Ed Blair/**Shostal/SuperStock;** 46, © **Hanover College;** 47, **North Wind Picture Archives;** 48, © **James P. Rowan;** 49, **Jefferson County Historical Society;** 50 (left), **Indiana State Library;** 50 (right), **AP/Wide World Photos;** 51, © **1989, Indianapolis Museum of Art, Gift of a Couple of Old Hoosiers;** 52-53, © **Cameramann International, Ltd.;** 55 (left), **Ball Corporation, Muncie;** 55 (right), **Indiana State Library;** 56, **Indiana State Library;** 57 (left), © Mark E. Gibson/**Marilyn Gartman Agency;** 57 (right), **AP/Wide World Photos;** 58, **Indiana Historical Society;** 59 (top left), © Greg L. Ryan-Sally Beyer/**Root Resources;** 59 (top right), **Studebaker Collection, Discovery Hall (Studebaker Museum, South Bend);** 59 (bottom), **Indiana State Library;** 60, **Amoco;** 61, **U.S. Steel, Inc.;** 62, **UPI/Bettmann Newsphotos;** 64 (both pictures), **Indiana State Library;** 65 (both pictures), **Roy Stryker Collection, University of Louisville Photo Archives;** 66, **AP/Wide World Photos;** 68, **UPI/Bettmann Newsphotos;** 69, **1987 WM Photography Services;** 70, © Georgia McGuire/**Journalism Services;** 72 (left), © J. C. Allen & Son, Inc./**Root Resources;** 72 (right), © **Cameramann International, Ltd.;** 74, © J. C. Allen & Son, Inc./**Root Resources;** 75 (left), © ABT/Bavaria/**H. Armstrong Roberts, Inc.;** 75 (right), © **Cameramann International, Ltd.;** 76, © J. C. Allen & Son, Inc./**Root Resources;** 77, © Andy Sacks/**TSW-Click/Chicago Ltd.;** 78-79, © **1989 Indianapolis Museum of Art, John Herron Fund;** 82 (left), **AP/Wide World Photos;** 82 (right), © Ed Kreminski/**Third Coast Stock Source;** 86 (both pictures), **AP/Wide World Photos;** 87, © **Michael K. Herbert;** 88, © Georgia McGuire/**Journalism Services;** 89 (left), © **Reinhard Brucker;** 89 (right), © Richard Fields/**Root Resources;** 90-91, **Shostal/SuperStock;** 93, © **Reinhard Brucker;** 94 (maps), **Len Meents;** 94 (right), © Cathlyn Melloan/**TSW-Click/Chicago Ltd.;** 95 (left), © **Reinhard Brucker;** 95 (right), © Cathlyn Melloan/**TSW-Click/Chicago Ltd.;** 97 (left), © Greg L. Ryan-Sally A. Beyer/**Root Resources;** 97 (map), **Len Meents;** 99 (left), © **Jeff Greenberg;** 99 (map), **Len Meents;** 101 (left), © J. C. Allen & Son, Inc./**Root Resources;** 101 (top right), © Ed Blair/**Shostal/SuperStock;** 101 (bottom right), © **Cathlyn Melloan;** 102 (left), © **Cathlyn Melloan;** 102 (right), © James F. Quinn/**Journalism Services;** 104 (map), **Len Meents;** 104 (right), © Cathlyn Melloan/**TSW-Click/Chicago Ltd.;** 107, © **James P. Rowan;** 108 (background), © Kitty Kohout/**Root Resources;** 108 (flag), **Courtesy Flag Research Center, Winchester, Massachusetts 01890;** 108 (flower), **H. Armstrong Roberts;** 108 (bird), © Anthony Mercieca/**Root Resources;** 111, © **Cathlyn Melloan;** 112, © **James P. Rowan;** 113 (left), © Skip Moody/**M. L. Dembinsky, Jr., Photography Associates;** 113 (top right), © Rod Planck/**M. L. Dembinsky, Jr., Photography Associates;** 113 (bottom right), © **Reinhard Brucker;** 116, **Shostal/SuperStock;** 117, © **Cathlyn Melloan;** 118 (left), **Auburn-Cord-Duesenberg Museum, Auburn, Indiana;** 118 (right), © Cathlyn Melloan/**TSW-Click/Chicago Ltd.;** 121, © Georgia McGuire/**Journalism Services;** 123, © Ed Blair/**Shostal/SuperStock;** 126 (both pictures), **AP/Wide World Photos;** 127 (Bird, Borman, and Carmichael), **AP/Wide World Photos;** 127 (Burnside), **Historical Pictures Service, Chicago;** 128 (Colfax and Harrison), **Historical Pictures Service, Chicago;** 128 (Debs and Grissom), **AP/Wide World Photos;** 129 (Hatcher), **UPI/Bettmann Newsphotos;** 129 (Hoffa), **Historical Pictures Service, Chicago;** 129 (Jackson and Lugar), **AP/Wide World Photos;** 130 (McQueen, Pauley, and Quayle), **AP/Wide World Photos;** 130 (Owen), **Historical Pictures Service, Chicago;** 131 (Rockne), **Historical Pictures Service, Chicago;** 131 (Samuelson, Stout, and Tharp), **AP/Wide World Photos;** 132, **Historical Pictures Service, Chicago;** 136, **Len Meents;** 138, © **Cathlyn Melloan;** 141, © Peter Pearson/**TSW-Click/Chicago Ltd.;** back cover, © Peter Pearson/**TSW-Click/Chicago Ltd.**